West Academic Publishing's Law School Advisory Board

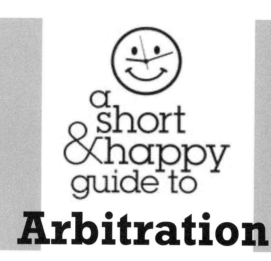

Arbitration

Henry Allen Blair
Robins Kaplan Distinguished Professor of Law
Senior Fellow, Dispute Resolution Institute
Mitchell Hamline School of Law

A SHORT & HAPPY GUIDE® SERIES

WEST
ACADEMIC
PUBLISHING

a short & happy guide series is a trademark registered in the U.S. Patent and Trademark Office.

© 2019 LEG, Inc. d/b/a West Academic

    444 Cedar Street, Suite 700
    St. Paul, MN 55101
    1-877-888-1330

Printed in the United States of America

ISBN: 978-1-64242-295-5

To Amanda Eiko Lindseth,
my sun, my moon, and all my stars.

Acknowledgments

There are far too many people to thank. It's inevitable that I'll leave someone essential out. So, I'll start by thanking everyone—you know who you are—who doesn't otherwise make it on this list.

First of all, my editor, Jon Harkness, made all this possible. Despite once upon a time having been a student of mine, he was generous enough to nevertheless help me get this project (and a bunch of others) off the ground, and I owe him an unpayable debt for it. Along those same lines, I'm giving a shout out to Louis Higgins and all of the wonderful staff and editors at West Academic. And, of course, I need to thank Paula Franzese who started the "Short and Happy" series.

I also need to thank to my mentor, friend, and co-author Thomas Carbonneau, without whom I would have never become interested in arbitration. And Kitty Atkins, without whom I would have never met Tom or gotten started in the dispute resolution field. Similarly, I need to thank a bunch of brilliant teachers, mentors, and colleagues who inspire and challenge me to keep learning: Loukas Mistelis, Robert Scott, Victor Goldberg, Anita Terry, Hon. Paul Magnuson, Hon. Jeffrey Bryan, Clifford Greene, Ania Farren, Marie Failinger, David Larson, Sharon Press, Carol Swanson, Steve Swanson, Jennifer Blair, Matt Vadnais, Liz Kramer, and Amanda Lindseth.

I owe a special thanks to my students, and particularly my arbitration students, who make teaching and writing so incredibly rewarding. And, in particular, I give a huge thanks to my research assistant, Beau RaRa, for making this book better.

Finally, but far from lastly, I would like to thank my family and friends, and in particular, Jillayne Berg, Ted Lindseth, and Frances Lindseth.

Table of Contents

A Short & Happy Guide to Arbitration

First Impressions and Introductions

You're interested in arbitration? Excellent! So am I!

In fact, I love teaching, writing, and thinking about arbitration, so I want to thank you for picking up this Short and Happy Guide.

Maybe you're a student taking a course related to arbitration, and you're looking for an edge to master the materials. Perhaps you're a lawyer who never took such a course, but you are now facing your first arbitration issue in practice. Maybe you're a business person or a business-mined person who realizes how foundational arbitration is to civil dispute resolution and you want to learn more. Or you might simply be a concerned citizen interested in the many commitments you have, even if you didn't understand you were making them, to arbitrate future disputes with your employer, cell phone provider, or supplier of just about every other consumer good you own or service you receive.

Whatever path has brought you to the subject, over the next 176 pages, I'm going to give you a conceptual map that will help guide you through the law, theory, and practice of arbitration.

Like all Short and Happy guides, this one doesn't cover every nuance or detail of the law. Arbitration can be bewildering because it involves a concoction of contract law, civil procedure, and constitutional law. It's one of those subjects that has equal parts fiddly doctrinal detail and big-picture policy. That's where this Guide comes in handy. It will not only orient you to the basic doctrine, but it will also give you the organization and tools you need to think through many arbitration problems.

In terms of scope, our primary focus will be the United States domestic law of arbitration, though Chapter 9 will introduce international commercial and state-investor arbitration, and I will reference, occasionally, the ways in which U.S. arbitration law is similar to or different from the domestic arbitration laws of other countries.

So, that's it for preliminaries. Without further ado, let's get this party started!

CHAPTER 1

What's Arbitration and How Does It Differ from Litigation and Other Forms of Dispute Resolution?

Arbitration derives its power from choice and commitment. In particular, arbitration constitutes the choice to opt-out of public courts and, instead, commit to have disputes adjudicated by private judges—arbitrators—picked by the parties.

Parties, in an increasingly wide and diverse range of transactional settings, are making that choice and commitment. In fact, you might not yet completely understand what arbitration is or how it functions, but you are almost certainly committed, whether you know it or not, to arbitrate a number of potential future disputes that you might have.

A savvy reader will note that this situation might not square with the "choice" part of things. After all, how could you have made a choice if you didn't understand what you were committing to do or choosing to give up? If you saw this, well done! You have put your finger on the key public policy issue in debates about disparate party arbitration. We'll return to this issue a number of times in this book, including in more detail in Chapter 8.

In the United States, a vast majority of consumer contracts with cellular phone companies, internet providers, internet search engines, retailers, travel companies, cable companies, and even utilities providers contain arbitration provisions. Pretty much all consumer contracts for goods include arbitration provisions. Moreover, as many as half of all non-unionized employment agreements contain mandatory arbitration provisions. If that wasn't enough, boilerplate in consumer or employment contracts may not be the only way that individuals could find themselves bound to an arbitration agreement. A couple of years ago, for instance, I went to a theatre in Los Angeles and noticed a sign stating that, by walking inside, I was agreeing to arbitrate any disputes that I might have with the owners of the joint.

Of course, arbitration exists in more than just consumer and employment contexts. In fact, arbitration constitutes a dominate force in all civil dispute resolution. Businesses arbitrate their fights with one another, both domestically and internationally. Investors arbitrate disagreements with the countries where they place their money. Governments arbitrate disputes with goods and services providers. Individuals arbitrate disputes with other individuals.

Depending on who you talk to, the prevalence of arbitration might be positive or negative or a little of both. Arbitration may be an ideal of freedom or a dangerous threat to shared society. Some see arbitration as allowing parties in conflict to focus a dispute resolution process on their actual lived needs rather than on abstracted and impersonal ideals of justice or, more cynically, on the procedural jockeying that serves only to line lawyers' pockets.

Others view arbitration as undermining the sanctity of the judicial system and thus of law itself. Still others see at least some forms of arbitration—arbitration imposed on weaker parties through boilerplate—as part of a scheme that results in the deletion of individuals' legal rights.

Whatever you ultimately conclude, an important goal of this book is to help you evaluate competing arguments in light of a comprehensive understanding of the nature and function of arbitration.

This Chapter introduces you to arbitration through a definition of its essential characteristics. It will then explore how arbitration has been used and has developed over time, distinguishing arbitration from other forms of dispute resolution. The Chapter then outlines, in broad strokes, the stages of the arbitral process.

1. What's Judge Judy Got to Do with It?: The Essential Characteristics of Arbitration

A. *The Essential Characteristics of Arbitration*

Judith Sheindlin was a judge—New York City Mayor Ed Koch appointed her to family court in 1982 and then made her Manhattan's supervising family court judge in 1986.[1] But she's no longer one. Despite the fact that she still wears a robe, presides over disputes in what appears to be a courtroom, works with a person called a "bailiff," and bangs a gavel, she's traded in her state-sanctioned judge powers for mere authority provided by the parties who appear before her. That said, she probably doesn't mind too terribly. She earns a tidy living as an arbitrator on her incredibly popular realty television show, Judge Judy— approximately $45 million a year!

---

[1] Interestingly, Mayor Koch went on, himself, to eventually "preside" over The People's Court from 1997-99.

To see why participants on Judge Judy are having their disputes decided in arbitration and not in a court, we need to develop a list of essential characteristics that all arbitrations share.

Fortunately, that list is pretty simple:

- Parties must voluntarily agree

- to give up their right to have their dispute adjudicated in a public court and

- instead to have an impartial third party

- issue a final and binding decision.

There are a few critical things to note.

First, arbitration amounts to a contract between the parties. The parties must voluntarily agree—choose—to resolve their dispute through arbitration or they will not be bound to arbitrate. As with any contract, a critical concern in arbitration law is ascertaining whether the parties have made that choice.[2] All the conventional defenses to contract formation, including lack of mutual assent, fraud, duress, and unconscionability, among others, apply to contracts for arbitration.

Second, the only essential characteristic that provides any semblance of how the arbitral process should be conducted is the requirement that the decision maker be impartial. That's it.

In fact, because contract rests at the core of arbitration, parties have extensive control over how the arbitrators are selected, what procedures the arbitrators must follow, and what remedial powers the arbitrators have. Put more simply, arbitrators

---

[2]   Some states have various forms of state-sanctioned, mandatory arbitration. For instance, it is common for states to have so-called "no-fault" statutes that require arbitrations of all cases where a motor vehicle accident victim seeks damages below some threshold, such as $10,000. *See, e.g.,* Minn. Stat. § 65B.525. But those statutes do not create "arbitration" for our purposes. The focus of this book is on binding arbitration as agreed to by the parties.

derive all of their power from the agreement of the parties, and the parties can do almost whatever they want in that agreement.

Third, arbitration must be final and binding. The "final" part means two things: the process must conclusively end the dispute and the parties have only one bite at the apple. When the arbitration is done, in other words, the parties' fight is done. There are no merits appeals. The binding part means what it sounds like: parties are committing to this one-shot process in lieu of going to a public court.

Finally, though it's maybe not entirely clear from this list, you should understand that labels aren't important. Judith Sheindlin calls herself a judge and the parties to disputes before her refer to her as one. But that doesn't matter. Whether a process constitutes "arbitration" or not has to be determined by the substance of the dispute resolution mechanism, not by the labels used by parties or arbitrators. A dispute resolution process called something other than "arbitration" may, in fact, be arbitration, so long as it meets the essential definitional criteria.

B. Wait, What? Entertainment as Adjudication?

You might have already known, before reading this, that Judge Judy and other television "judges" are not really judges. After all, they never seem too bothered by rules of evidence or procedure or even proper judicial decorum. They make snap decisions, often with few facts, and they apply only threadbare (and frequently wrong) law. Sometimes my students think that these shows are completely rigged and that the parties are paid actors. But that's not accurate either. Usually, at least, these shows do center on real disputes. Participants agree to have their fight adjudicated by Judge Judy, giving her freedom to issue a decision based on whatever rationale she thinks appropriate, in front of a televised audience, and they agree that her decision will be final and binding.

Accordingly, court television seems to meet the essential definitional criteria to be arbitration. Most courts that have considered the matter agree. But if you're like me, there's something about this conclusion that just doesn't quite feel right. It's worth pausing for a moment to consider why.

Does the fact that these disputes are decided primarily for entertainment purposes undermine the credibility or sanctity of the process as a serious method of resolving a dispute? Does that, or should that, matter? Does it alter your thinking to learn that, if the plaintiff wins, the show's producers pay the award and, if the defendant wins, both parties get an "appearance fee?" Might not this system skew things in favor of the defendants, incentivizing them to take their case from court to TV? If they have a weak case, appearing on the show absolves them of any financial liability, and if they have a strong case, they can earn an appearance fee along with their victory. Basically, defendants never lose. Can there be an adjudication without a loser? (Note that plaintiffs can win, so maybe that's sufficient?)

It's worth asking these sorts of big-think questions regularly when ruminating about arbitration. In Chapters 3 and 8, we'll consider the minimal requirements of procedural due process in arbitration, but I always tell my students that, at some gut level, I believe everyone agrees that the essential criteria for arbitration may not be entirely sufficient. The arbitral process may need to guarantee more. It may be, in other words, that to qualify as arbitration, we expect a process to bear at least some of the hallmarks of a serious and responsible adjudicatory system.

All that said, interesting questions are just that, interesting questions. A key recurring theme of this book will be that courts, especially in the U.S., generously construe processes and agreements in favor of arbitration. When in doubt, courts kick a case out and send it to arbitration.

2. A Really, Really, Really Brief History of Arbitration

As the OK Go sing (in *White Knuckles*, if you're interested) "nothing' ever doesn't change, but nothin' changes much." You could do worse in trying to find a single sentence to sum up the history of arbitration.

Commentators debate various possible origins of arbitration. Aristotle, for instance, refers to arbitration in his Rhetoric. Citizens in ancient Athens, for a period of time, became eligible for appointment as an arbitrator when they retired from military service at the age of 60. Public lists of these eligible arbitrators have survived to this day. Records also exist indicating that it was a goal among at least some Romans to put an end to litigation by means of arbitration. Additionally, references to arbitration can be found in the Quran and the ethical teachings of the Mahabharata.

Stories of origins, however, are frequently more complicated than they at first seem. While possessing certain features of what we would think of as arbitration, the relationships between these ancient forms of adjudication and various other judicial mechanisms were intricate.

For our purposes, it's enough to say that arbitration is old. Really old. Like, it is the oldest consistent form of adjudication that the world has ever known.

What's probably more useful than rehearsing the nuances of arbitration law through the ages, fun as that could be, is a brief look at the more recent history of the subject. (You might object as you read the next couple of paragraphs that my definition of "recent" and yours are very different. But bear with me. I'll keep this short and happy, I promise.)

A pretty modern version of arbitration has been a feature of dispute resolution at least since the fourteenth century. Early forms of arbitration were created and administered by trade groups—merchant or producer communities. These groups established norms of conduct and business standards for their members, and they empaneled the most respected folks in the community as decision makers.

By the seventeenth century, it was common to have mercantile disputes resolved by arbitration run by merchant and craft guilds themselves. Merchant and craft guilds established arbitration tribunals because they felt that the courts weren't sufficiently knowledgeable about commercial customs and often relied on rarified legal principles that had little or nothing to do with the daily stuff important to them. Moreover, courts were slow and cumbersome. Arbitration tribunals, in contrast, were composed of experts in the trade who applied the very usages and practices that really mattered.

There's something worth highlighting about this more modern history: arbitration focused on disputes in particular commercial communities. It wasn't an all-purpose dispute resolution process. That does not mean that it wasn't occasionally used in other situations. In fact, George Washington served as an arbiter of private disputes before the Revolution, and incorporated the following provision in his will:

> I hope and trust, that no disputes will arise concerning [the devises in this will]; but if, contrary to expectation, of the usual technical terms, or because too much or too little has been said on any of the Devises to be consonant with law, My Will and direction expressly is, that all disputes (if unhappily any should arise) shall be decided by three impartial and intelligent men, known for their probity and understanding, two to be chosen by the disputants—each having a choice of one—and the third by those two. Which three men thus chosen, shall,

> unfettered by Law, or legal constructions; declare their
> Sense of the Testator's intention; and such decision is, to
> all intents and purposes to be as binding on the Parties as
> if it had been given in the Supreme Court of the United
> States.[3]

But the modern foundations of arbitration are firmly rooted in commercial disputes.

In the context of commercial disputes, arbitration worked pretty great. Merchants and craft guilds seemed content with it. But courts, especially in the United States in the late nineteenth and early twentieth centuries, were not fans. Arbitration remained outside of and in tension with the legal system. Courts, in fact, were skeptical of any efforts by parties to customize their dispute resolution procedures, including through things that are quite common today like choice of law provisions, choice of forum or venue provisions, waivers of service of process, and other similar party agreements. Courts saw such private agreements about procedure as dangerous threats to the legitimate public function of the judiciary. With respect to arbitration contracts, Courts would not grant specific performance as a remedy for breach because they said agreements to arbitrate were revocable by either party until the arbitral award was rendered.

One of the clearest and most frequently quoted explanations of this approach comes from the Supreme Court of the United States in *Home Insurance Co. v. Morse*:

> [a] man may not barter away his life or his freedom,
> [sic] or his substantial rights [including the right to go to
> court]. . . . He cannot . . . bind himself in advance by an
> agreement [to arbitrate], which may be specifically

---

[3]   NORDHAM, GEORGE WASHINGTON AND MONEY 201 (1982).

enforced, thus to forfeit his rights at all times and on all occasions, whenever the case may be presented.

In the Court's view, privately negotiated contract provisions could not trump the role of the public adjudicatory system. If such contract provisions were enforced, the "regular administration of justice might be greatly impeded . . . ."[4]

Attitudes towards arbitration began to change, however, with rapid economic transformations in the American economy in the twentieth century. Businesses saw potential efficiency gains from arbitration, but they were frustrated with court refusal to enforce arbitration agreements. Calls for the legal system to value freedom of contract fueled a reform effort. As Julius Henry Cohen, the chief draftsman of the Federal Arbitration Act, explained, "everybody today feels very strongly that the right of freedom of contract which the Constitution guarantees [to people] . . . includes the right to dispose of any controversy which may arise out of the contract in their own fashion."[5]

Responding to the interests of the business community, in 1920, New York broke from traditional law and enacted a statute that enforced pre-dispute agreements to arbitrate. The statute ended the practice of courts hearing questions of law during the course of arbitration and provided for only limited judicial review of final awards. In 1925, the U.S. Congress followed New York's lead by enacting the United States Arbitration Act, later renamed the Federal Arbitration Act or, as we'll call it from here on out, the FAA.

The FAA ushered in a new path for merchants and craft guild members to enforce their arbitration agreements, but the Act

---

    [4]   87 U.S. 445 (1874).

    [5]   *Arbitration of Interstate Commercial Disputes: Joint Hearings Before the Subcomms. of the Comms. on the Judiciary on S. 1005 and H.R. 646*, 68th Cong. 14 (1924) (statement of Julius Henry Cohen).

remained, effectively, a special interest piece of legislation until the 1960s. At that point, the Supreme Court of the United States decided, for reasons that we'll discuss in other parts of this book, that it really, really, really loved arbitration. And, so the contemporary law of arbitration in the United States was born.

Today, arbitration has far outgrown its merchant and craft guild roots. It has become *a* primary, if not *the* primary, mechanism by which civil disputes are adjudicated in the United States.

It's also worth mentioning that arbitration has taken on a rapidly growing significance internationally. Particularly in transborder business transactions, arbitration has become the key mechanism for resolving disputes. There are several reasons for this growth, which we'll discuss in Chapter 9, but maybe the most significant is something called the Convention on the Recognition and Enforcement of Foreign Arbitral Awards (the New York Convention). This international treaty has entered into force in 159 countries as of 2018, and it effectively makes enforcing an international commercial arbitral award as easy as enforcing a domestic court judgment in signatory countries. No analogue to the New York Convention exists for enforcing a judicial judgment across international borders.

3. Apples, Oranges, and Guavas: Comparing Arbitration to Other Modes of Dispute Resolution

Dispute resolution aims to end the dispute. Certainly, other goals are part of the equation, like maintaining or fostering relationships, vindicating rights, deterring wrongdoing, compensating victims, and so forth. But the second word in the phrase "dispute resolution" makes clear that putting an end to the fight matters.

Still, there are a lot of ways to end a fight. Dispute resolution, then, exists along a spectrum. At the least formal end sits direct, party-to-party negotiation. On this end, parties try to settle their own disputes. At the other, most formal end sits a trial in public court. On this end, a judge makes a final decision about the dispute that binds the parties. In between these poles are a number of processes that differ in significant ways.

A. A Summary Comparison of Dispute Resolution Processes

Let's start by considering the two poles more closely.

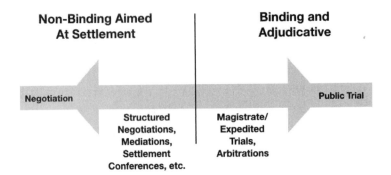

Direct, party-to-party negotiation gives the disputants maximum control over the process and its outcome. But it also provides no structure within which the resolution occurs. For that reason, it offers very little protection to either side. There are no procedures to follow, no outsiders provide guidance or oversight, no rights mandate an outcome, and nothing but the constraints of generally applicable law protect either party from strong-arm tactics. One party, in other words, can't punch the other in the face or engage in similar sorts of tortious or criminal misconduct, but that's about it. The parties can agree on whatever outcome or resolution they want, subject only to the limits of contract law and public policy to enforce that arrangement. Or, they can fail to reach an agreement and move on with other forms of dispute resolution.

On the other hand, trial in a public court gives the parties significantly less control over the process used to resolve a dispute, and parties have very limited ability to control the outcome. But trials strive to give both sides a level playing field on which they present their case to a neutral decision maker (or decision makers, when juries are involved) who proclaim a winner and a loser based on a set of legal rights. The process relies on detailed rules of procedure and evidence, and an expert in both—the judge—retains control. This formality functions to assure each side a reasonably fair and equal opportunity to have their grievances and arguments heard. Parties who are still adjudicating in public court are free to settle, of course, but the result of any adjudication will be binding on them, subject only to any right of appeal.

Conventionally, processes along the spectrum between these poles are divided into two classifications: "non-binding" processes aimed at reaching an agreed upon settlement or "adjudicative" processes aimed at a binding and final resolution of the dispute.

Non-binding processes take place in the "shadow" of adjudicative processes. In other words, parties engaged in one of the non-binding processes know that they may always opt to resolve a dispute in a more formal and adjudicative way. The overhang of that possibility impacts the behaviors and decisions of parties to non-binding processes.

On the other hand, the ultimate ability of parties to settle their dispute, even on the eve of a final decision by a judge or arbitrator in an adjudicative process means that non-binding processes also exert a tremendous influence over the course of an adjudication.

So, where's arbitration fit into all this? Well, it's similar to other less formal processes like negotiation or mediation in that it lets the parties to a dispute choose the procedural hoops they would rather skip in exchange for a speedy resolution. And, parties to an arbitration typically keep their dispute private, pick their decision maker, and exercise a lot more control over how the process functions. Accordingly, while distinct from mediation and negotiation, arbitration shares some of the same pre-legal intuitions and roots.

Unlike mediation and negotiation, however, arbitration is an adjudicative process. Like a trial in a public court, a decision maker issues a final and binding decision, declaring a winner and a loser on each issue. It is, therefore, an adversarial process.

The following table lays out some rough and generalized differences between three of the most emblematic dispute resolution processes.

Mediation	Arbitration	Public Trial
Conceptual and holistic	More rule based	Rule based
Collaborative and often creative	Adversarial and more analytical	Adversarial and analytical
Non-binding	Binding	Binding
Aimed at promoting agreement	Zero-sum adjudication, with a winner and a loser on each issue	Zero-sum adjudication, with a winner and a loser on each issue
Mediator is usually paid by the parties	Arbitrator is paid by the parties	Judge is paid by the government
Mediator is usually paid by the hour or by the case by the parties	Arbitrator is usually paid by the hour or by the case by the parties	Judge is paid a salary by the government

Mediation	Arbitration	Public Trial
Mediator does not render a binding opinion at all and rarely expresses an opinion about the merits	Arbitrator renders a final and binding decision that may be based on law but could also be based on expertise, industry norms, or equities	Judge renders a final and binding decision based on law
No Jury	No Jury	Sometimes a Jury
No rules of procedure	Informal rules of procedure	Formal rules of procedure
Private and confidential	Private and usually confidential	Public
No appeal, but it's not binding	No appeal and limited judicial review	Appeal as a matter of right

B. The Prevalence of Arbitration in Comparison to Other Dispute Resolution Processes

Though arbitration is just one of a number of dispute resolution methods, it has become less an "alternative" form of adjudication and more the norm for many civil disputes.

Significantly, arbitration exists everywhere in the modern United States, but it has not replaced other non-adjudicative methods of dispute resolution, like mediation. Instead, the rise of arbitration and these other out-of-court modes of resolving disputes means that there are fewer cases in public courts. Arbitration, in other words, constitutes one substitute for courts.

There are many potential reasons for explosive growth of arbitration and other alternatives to court. At least partly, however, the growth is an indictment of the court system. Legal traffic jams caused by bloated court dockets limit access to justice for many people and businesses. Litigation in courts can be crowded, slow and expensive. Arbitration avoids the problem, scooting cases into the fast lane and shaving months or even years off the wait time for a resolution.

But the allure of arbitration goes deeper than just that it's fast. Court congestion can make it difficult for judges to be as focused on civil cases as parties might like. Remember, judges are busy generalists, with criminal cases, family law cases, juvenile cases, probate cases, and civil cases of all shapes and sizes vying for their attention. Additionally, although the ideal of a jury trial still holds some sway, the number of cases decided by juries at both the state and federal level has been declining sharply and consistently for more than fifty years. Anyway, even when they are used, juries are notoriously unpredictable. The potential of rogue juries or judges without the time to invest in understanding complex or technical facts makes public court dispute resolution costlier in many instances. Arbitration, in contrast, offers the parties control over who the decision maker will be, giving them greater ability calibrate the decision maker's knowledge, expertise, and schedule to the needs of the particular case.

Internationally, arbitration constitutes the most effective and efficient means of resolving cross-border disputes, not least because it is much easier to enforce an arbitral award in a distant country than it is to enforce a foreign court's judgment.

All this makes arbitration sound pretty darned good. And often it is. But there's more to the story.

There are sobering reasons to be skeptical of at least some forms of arbitration. In recent years, in fact, arbitration has come under heavy scrutiny. Many employee and consumer rights advocates, scholars, journalists, and politicians are worried about what they see as a dangerous privatization of justice. Arbitration may be well and fine when power remains relatively balanced between the parties—commercial disputes between businesses, for instance. But parties with little or no bargaining power who are forced into arbitration agreements buried in boilerplate that they didn't see, read, or understand raise different concerns. The stronger party may be able to skew the process so far in its advantage as to dilute or outright delete the rights of the weaker party.

4. The Many Faces of Arbitration: Stages of the Arbitral Process

Like the socks my twin sisters-in-law wear, no two arbitrations match one another. That shouldn't be too surprising because, as you've seen, arbitration takes place in a wide variety of contexts. What's more, the parties have great latitude to customize the process to meet their particular needs, so each arbitration can be truly unique. It's beyond the scope of this Guide to examine the internal procedures that parties might adopt in any detail, so the point here is to see the big picture—the lifecycle of an arbitration. Essentially, arbitrations have six broad stages:

- The parties agree to arbitrate a particular dispute;

- The parties proceed to arbitration or one of them resists and the other must compel arbitration;

- The parties choose an arbitrator (or arbitrators);

- The parties prepare for and participate in the arbitral hearing;

- The arbitrators issue an award; and

- The parities comply with the award or one of them resists and the other must seek judicial aid to enforce it.

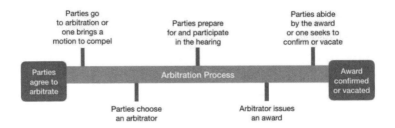

A. The Parties Agree to Arbitrate

There can be no arbitration without an agreement. Without the choice to opt out of public courts and instead commit to resolve a dispute in arbitration, the parties are not bound, and the arbitrator has no power.

So, the first step in an arbitration is finding the parties' agreement to arbitrate a particular dispute.

- The agreement to arbitrate may appear in an arbitral clause or a submission.

- The agreement must be in writing.

- The agreement must satisfy the general requirements of contract law.

- The particular dispute between the parties must be covered by the agreement to arbitrate.

Typically, parties agree to arbitrate in what we'll call an arbitral clause. We'll call it a "clause" because it's merely one of a number of provisions contained in some bigger contract. For instance, imagine a contract between Blair, an author, and West, a publisher. That contract will contain a number of provisions governing things like copyright ownership, deadlines, quality and editing requirements, royalties, and a bunch of other substantive provisions. One of the clauses in the contract, however, might commit the parties to arbitrate all future potential disputes between them. We can call the bigger contract a "container contract" because it contains this arbitral clause.

In an arbitral clause, parties choose arbitration for the resolution of future disputes between them. At the time that they enter into the container contract, Blair and West are not in conflict. Instead, they are hopefully looking forward to a mutually beneficial and rewarding relationship. But the course of true love never did run smooth. Conflicts can and do arise, so lawyers for parties include a dispute resolution provision that establishes the rules of the game if things go south.

Now imagine for a moment that Blair and West didn't include a dispute resolution clause in their container contract. Can they choose, after a dispute has arisen, to arbitrate? Of course they can! Such a post-dispute agreement to arbitrate is called a "submission."

Submissions are less common, probably because parties are already fighting, so it's difficult for them to agree on anything, let alone on the procedure they want to use to resolve their dispute. But, in theory, nothing prevents a submission.

Whether in the form of an arbitral clause or a submission, one of the few formalities imposed by the law of arbitration is that the agreement must be in writing. That said, courts have taken an increasingly liberal view of what constitutes a sufficient writing. At this point, courts are pretty willing to aggregate multiple writings, and courts usually accept any recorded data as a writing (emails, texts, and even voice mails).

Beyond the formal requirement of a writing, the arbitration agreement must qualify as a contract for purposes of general contract law. Chapter 6 will review those requirements in the context of arbitration.

Finally, the particular dispute between the parties must be subject to arbitration under the agreement. The dispute, in other words, must be arbitrable. Chapters 3 and 6 address this issue.

B. The Parties Proceed to Arbitration or One of Them Resists and the Other Must Compel Arbitration

Much of the time, parties follow through on their promises. Promises to arbitrate are no exception.

But sometimes, as can happen with any promise, a party might have what I call "regretsies." Contract law, in a nutshell, addresses the problem of regretsies. The whole point of contract law is to make some promises legally enforceable, meaning that the law will require a party who made but now regrets a promise to keep it or pay for breaching it.

Because an arbitration agreement amounts to just a kind of contract, the problem of regretsies exists. If a party has chosen to give up the right to resolve a dispute in a public court and instead promised to arbitrate, arbitration law addresses the problem by forcing the reluctant party to follow through on its commitment.

Specifically, if one party to a valid and binding arbitration agreement refuses to arbitrate, the other party can go to a public court and bring a motion to compel arbitration. Chapter 6 will address such motions, but for now it's enough to say that they are really seeking a remedy for a breach of the arbitration contract. Compelling arbitration is a form of specific performance—a remedy that forces a breaching party to actually do what that party promised to do.

It's worth pausing for a moment to think about this. Most of the time, at least in the U.S., a party that breaches a contract merely has to pay money damages. So why can't a party who breaches a promise to arbitrate merely pay money damages?

Well, what would those damages be? There are a lot of different and complex reasons the non-breaching party might have wanted to arbitrate. So, what is monetary value of that party's harm if the other refuses to arbitrate? Putting a dollar value on that harm could be quite difficult and would require its own, separate lawsuit, apart from and in addition to the original fight!

Arbitration law skips that whole mess and provides a simple and direct remedy: force the non-performing party to do as she promised—arbitrate.

This basic idea remains at play even if things get more procedurally complicated. Imagine, for instance that Alejo, an entrepreneur, entered into a contract with Pests-R-Us selling the company valuable intellectual property rights in a better mouse trap. In the container contract, the parties included a broad arbitration clause committing them to arbitrate "any and all future disputes."

Pests-R-Us now believes that Alejo has violated the terms of the contract by selling a better rat trap to a competitor, so it files a lawsuit in a public court. By doing this, Pests-R-Us has effectively refused to arbitrate, as it promised to do. Alejo can bring a motion to compel Pests-R-Us to go to arbitration. But what about the pending public court case?

To vindicate Alejo's right to have the dispute heard in arbitration, the court must not only compel Pests-R-Us to follow through on its promise to arbitrate, but it must stay (or dismiss) the pending public court case. And that is precisely what arbitration law requires. Again, the details of this stay (or dismissal) right will be discussed in detail in Chapter 6. It's enough to understand, for now, that this stay (or dismissal) right constitutes an adjunct remedy to the remedy of compelling a reluctant party to go to arbitration.

C. *The Parties Choose an Arbitrator (or Arbitrators)*

In many respects, the arbitrator is the arbitration. Until an arbitrator has been appointed, the arbitration cannot really begin, though some institutions do allow for emergency procedures that precede appointment of an arbitrator.

The details of selecting and appointing an arbitrator can vary greatly. Although there are many possible methods of actually selecting an arbitrator, the parties get to choose a method and often have significant or complete power to pick an arbitrator.

Commonly, arbitrations are conducted by one or three arbitrators, depending on what the parties want. Having more arbitrators means that the parties can involve decision makers with differing areas of expertise. But it also means that the arbitration becomes much more expensive. If the parties opt to have a panel with three arbitrators, it is conventional for each party to select one arbitrator and then for the party-selected arbitrators to agree on a third arbitrator who will serve as the chair of the proceeding.

Issues in selection can arise if the parties have a deadlock. If the parties' agreement does not provide a means of resolving such deadlocks, arbitration law effectively allows a court to appoint an arbitrator on behalf of the parties.

D. *The Parties Prepare for and Participate in the Arbitral Hearing*

Parties present their case to the arbitrator who will evaluate arguments and evidence in order to render a decision. This takes place at a hearing.

The arbitral hearing often functions like a less formalized trial, but this need not be true. Rather than being a culminating event in the lifecycle of the adjudication, like a trial, hearings may occur episodically. Parties and arbitrators can fashion the process of gathering and presenting evidence in novel ways best tailored to meet the needs of a given case. They can forgo time-consuming and costly technicalities, streamline processes, and stage presentation of evidence and arguments in whatever order makes sense. There's no need to be hampered by pre-fabricated procedures.

Still, much of the time, the process does in fact work somewhat like a public court trial. Often, there's some sort of pre-hearing conference or conferences, during which the parties address preliminary issues, like the arbitrator's jurisdiction, the location of the hearing, preliminary relief, choice of law, and the bounds of what information gathering or discovery will be allowed. Commonly, the process continues through information gathering or discovery, which leads to some sort of summary adjudication motion, similar to a summary judgment in a public court. The process then concludes with a final hearing, during which parties may make arguments and present witness testimony, frequently through attorneys acting as their advocates.

E. *The Arbitrators Issue an Award*

When the arbitrators have come to a decision, they will create an award. Unless the parties have otherwise agreed, the award doesn't need to include written explanations or justifications for the decision. But, as a matter of practice, more and more arbitration awards include at least some explanation or rationale.

The rendering of the final award triggers the parties' obligations to pay the arbitrator's fees, though, in practice many arbitrators (and institutions) require the parties to pay incrementally throughout the process.

At last, the final award ends the arbitration. Once the award has been rendered, the arbitrator's function and power ends and so too does the power of the parties to control the process. There's a fancy Latinate name for this moment—*functus officio*. It means that the official function of the arbitrator has ended or concluded.

F. The Parties Comply with the Award or a Party Resists and the Other Must Seek Judicial Aid to Enforce It

Parties frequently comply with arbitration awards, just as they do with arbitration agreements in the first place. If parties voluntarily agree to abide by an award, no judicial action is needed. But, of course, parties, or one of them, might not be satisfied with the award or the process.

Enforcement of arbitral awards will be discussed in detail in Chapter 7. The upshot is that a court may wind up reviewing the award. Importantly, any such review will be limited under arbitration law to a very narrow set of grounds. Basically, a court will be looking to make sure that there was a valid agreement to arbitrate and that the process satisfied the minimal criteria for procedural due process—the arbitrators were impartial, they didn't engage in misconduct, they gave the parties a reasonably equal opportunity to be heard, and they observed the authority given to them by the parties in the arbitration agreement. It's vital to see that none of these grounds involves a court looking through the process to the merits of the dispute. Courts do not and cannot conduct a merits review of the arbitrators' decision.

That's so important that I'll put it in a separate paragraph and repeat it: Courts do not and cannot conduct a merits review of the arbitrators' decision.

This means that no mechanism exists to correct substantive errors by the arbitrators. (There may be a very, very, very limited exception to this, discussed in Chapter 7.) In public courts, such errors are corrected, at least in theory, by the appellate process. There are no appeals of arbitration awards.

> *This is something of an overstatement. Some arbitral institutions do have "appellate-like" optional rules that parties may agree to use in their arbitration agreements. But these processes are still within arbitration. They do not give public courts any ability to conduct a merits review of the process.*

If an award is "confirmed," arbitration law converts the award into a public court judgment enforceable like any other judgment of a court. If the award is overturned—"vacated" in the terminology of arbitration—what happens next will depend on what the reason for the vacatur was. Basically, if the reviewing court concludes that there was no valid arbitration agreement, then the parties will have to resolve their dispute in public court. If the reviewing court vacates the award on any other basis, the parties will probably have to restart the arbitration from scratch.

CHAPTER 2

Pros and Cons: Assessing When Arbitration Works Best

Sometimes there's no right answer, but there are often wrong ones. With respect to the choice about whether to arbitrate or litigate in a public court, this adage can come in handy. Often the best decision hinges on there being a clear reason *not* to litigate or a clear reason *not* to arbitrate.

I think of it this way: selection of a dispute resolution process usually occurs before any dispute has festered. At that stage, assuming neither party has a time-turner (Harry Potter reference, in case you don't know),[1] neither party knows for sure what they might fight about or what the facts of a fight will be.

That shared nescience allows the parties to be more thoughtful. They are not yet inflamed by the passions that arise after a conflict has erupted. And they both have an incentive to

---

[1] My research assistant insisted that I include a note explaining that I am a proud Slytherin. You can find out what house you're from, if you haven't already, by taking a wonderful quiz on Pottermore—https://www.pottermore.com.

think about designing a process that will be fair no matter what side of the facts they might wind up with.

It's like the old trick that parents use to solve cake problems.

Inevitably, with two children around, a time will come when there's one last piece of cake and both kids want it. Clever parents will foresee the possibility of future strife and preemptively get the kids to agree to a process for resolving it. They'll tell the children that, in such a future struggle, one of them will cut the cake and the other will have the right to choose which piece she wants. The benefits of the system become obvious. If the cutter cheats and makes one piece bigger, the chooser will reap the advantages. This incentivizes the cutter to be as equal as possible in the division.

But this equitable solution works best if the kids are uncertain which position they might ultimately occupy. In an actual dispute, for instance, one of the children may feel that she has been wronged because she didn't get her fair share of the rest of the cake. She's entitled to the entire last piece!

The lack of information about what the future might hold, in short, makes it easier to get the kids to agree on a dispute resolution process but it also means that they might commit to a process that they come to regret once they understand the facts of an actual fight. What looked like a good idea before a dispute might, in light of the actual conflict, seem like a really bad one.

Unfortunately, as concerning as this mismatch between expectations and reality could be, no dispute resolution mechanism can fix it. No system can guarantee that it will be both desirable before a dispute arises and after one has fomented. Accordingly, as you review these pros and cons of arbitration, keep in mind that selection of a dispute resolution process requires thoughtful appraisal of a variety of factors, but at the end of the day, no system will be ideal in all situations.

Additionally, when thinking about the various pros and cons of arbitration, it's important to remember that, at this point in history, arbitration occupies a central place in dispute resolution, especially in the United States. As we will discuss in more detail in Chapters 3 and 4, virtually any matter of civil dispute can be arbitrated, and federal law ensures that states have essentially no role in policing arbitration.

So, with almost no hard stops on what can be arbitrated, the decision to arbitrate or not truly is a matter of efficiency and preference.

1. Some Pros

A. Pro: Arbitration Is Cheaper (Maybe?)

Time is money. To the extent that's true, arbitration may, in fact, be cheaper than public court litigation.

Like any form of adjudication, parties may, of course, cease the process by settling their dispute. That's as true in arbitration as in public court litigation. Holding that option constant, arbitration may well be faster.

It might not be entirely accurate to say that settlements happen as frequently in arbitration as they do in public court litigation. If arbitration costs less, settlement might not be as likely. With lower process costs hanging over the parties' heads, parties might prefer to adjudicate the dispute to resolution rather than fully settle. All that said, examining whether full settlements are socially more desirable than a completed adjudication would not be a short or happy exploration. It's worth nothing, though, that the question may not be as self-evident as it at first seems.

Arbitration promises the potential of case-specific customization and relative informality—including less discovery than court litigation and simplified rules of evidence. These features should speed things up. Additionally, parties can use arbitration to avoid a backlog of previously filed public court cases thereby jumping to a quicker outcome. Finally, lack of an appeals process should regularly make arbitration faster than public court litigation. While arbitration awards can be challenged in court, the grounds for setting aside an award are much more limited than the grounds for reversing a trial court's decision and, most importantly, there is no merits review of an arbitral award in court.

Still, while arbitration may be faster, the empirical evidence remains inconclusive about whether it's actually cheaper. Most experienced arbitration lawyers tell clients that it's not. Arbitration has systematic costs associated with it that are likely to increase expense, at least in the short run. Most significantly, these costs include the fees charged by the arbitrator or arbitrators and, if one is used, an arbitral institution. In fact, as discussed in a moment, arbitration might be attractive to parties precisely because arbitrators are experts in the field, but expertise isn't cheap. Fees of arbitrators vary greatly but could be anywhere between $250-$1,500 an hour (or more). In comparison, parties do not pay for the services of public court judges, at least directly. (They pay, but they do so through the diffuse process of taxes that we all share.)

B. Pro: Flexibility (if Parties Use It?)

Arbitration extends the flexibility that parties have in agreeing what they will do to how they will resolve fights about whether they did it or not.

The one-size-fits-all procedural rules in public courts might not be optimal in all circumstances. Arbitration allows parties to negotiate over the contents not only of their substantive obligations but also of their preferred enforcement mechanisms. In other words, arbitration allows parties to use the dispute resolution process to limit the risks of adjudication and even create additional incentives for performance.

For instance, parties may adjust the timing and other pedestrian aspects of the adjudication, making the process work for them instead of having to meet the scheduling needs of a judge. These sorts of seemingly minor customizations can pay huge dividends, reducing costs (not just in terms of money but in terms of time and inconvenience) by allowing the parties to disperse their dispute resolution obligations sensibly, avoiding what can be an expensive bunching or inefficient overlap of deadlines. But parties can go further in flexibly tailoring the arbitral process to meet their unique needs.

Parties could, for example, agree that expert testimony will be given by a neutral third party whose fee is paid jointly by the parties rather than through party-appointed advocates, as would occur in a public court. This sort of process for expert testimony would not only be more cost effective, but it could incentivize greater compliance with the performance requirements of a contract. If parties know before a dispute arises that they will have an agreed-upon expert looking over their shoulder if they arguably violate their substantive commitments, they might behave better. At the least, such a system could change the parties' calculus in deciding what claims to bring and how much to invest in proving claims once they have been asserted.

You can imagine all sorts of other customizations. An almost infinite number of options exists. The point is that agreement about how future disputes will be adjudicated can bracket the risks or costs of litigation and positively influence parties' behavior during performance of the contract.

Despite these possible benefits, what little empirical evidence that we have suggests that parties may not often use the full flexibility arbitration offers. That begs the question of just how valuable such flexibility actually might be to parties.

C. Pro: Expert Adjudicators

You may have heard of forum shopping? Or perhaps you've heard of judge-shopping? Usually, these concepts get a bad rap. Our system of public courts strives to avoid forum shopping and judge shopping, resting on the belief that justice can be best served by having a complete stranger to a situation resolve a dispute.

Arbitration rests on a different belief. In fact, one of the most foundational ideas in arbitration is that insiders know more about the facts and circumstances that matter to disputing parties than do strangers.

I think of it this way: my wife has a brother. They have, since they were young, had a loving but competitive relationship. Back in the mists of history, their parents purchased a holiday decoration for their Christmas tree—a kind of gaudy walnut. It has come to be known as the "Xmas Walnut." For reasons that remain entirely unclear to me, my wife and her brother coveted the right to place the Xmas Walnut on the tree. In an act that I can only imagine as hotly contested mediation, their parents got them to agree, when they were both of single digit ages, to a complicated process by which the rights to place the Xmas Walnut are determined each new year. That process has been augmented and revised, ever so slightly, over the years and is not written down. Effectively, the process involves a variety of situation-specific factors hinging on stuff that has occurred in the current year. To this day, however, the rights to place the Xmas Walnut are valued greatly by my wife and her brother.

Imagine that my wife and her brother have a dispute about the outcome of the complicated process by which their rights are determined. Who would they want to resolve that dispute? A stranger who hasn't the slightest clue what all the fuss is about or someone who knows the people involved and has a close understanding of the practices?

I think that if an outsider were to hear a dispute between them, that outsider would screw things up royally. Not only would the outsider mistake how seriously my wife and her brother (and the family) take this seemingly ridiculous ritual, but the outsider would have no sense of the practices at issue. But, someone who has seen the process work, gets that this is not just some silly tradition but something that has become legitimately important to them and their family—and can look past formalisms to see how the process has actually functioned over the years—would be far better suited to resolve the dispute.

That's the instinct behind arbitration. In fact, perhaps one of the most significant reasons parties might choose arbitration over judicial litigation is because they want decision makers with experience in the relevant business or practice. Adjudicators with expertise and experience may bolster the efficiency benefits of arbitration. A tribunal consisting of industry experts could have familiarity with key legal precedents, understand trade usages and practices, and be able to evaluate complicated facts more adroitly and without need for additional expert testimony by partisan witnesses. Accordingly, the space within which expensive and opportunistic post-dispute tactical maneuvering take place can be limited in arbitration.

Expert adjudicators may also provide more accurate and balanced decisions, being better equipped to understand the sector-specific law and facts at issue in a dispute. Indeed, good evidence exists that businesses often choose arbitration precisely because they want to avoid excessive, emotionally driven or erratic jury awards. Arbitrators might be more likely than juries or even public court judges to understand business needs and circumstances and better positioned to make properly calibrated judgments.

D. Pro: Privacy/Confidentiality (Though This Could Be a Big Con Too)

Privacy or confidentiality may be another key reason for parties to choose arbitration over judicial litigation.

Arbitration usually takes place behind closed doors. The public is not invited or allowed to watch. For example, Rule 25 of the American Arbitration Association ("AAA") provides that "[t]he arbitrator and the AAA shall maintain the privacy of the hearings" and further provides that the arbitrator shall have the power to exclude anyone who is not "essential" to the proceeding. Moreover, awards generally are not published. Unless the parties to the arbitration agree to disclose information, or a court commands that information be divulged, competitors, clients, and business associates ordinarily have no knowledge of the dispute, the proceedings, or the outcome.

Parties can also easily impose stricter and more formal confidentiality requirements on the arbitral process. For instance, the Revised Uniform Arbitration Act allows the arbitrator to issue protective orders when necessary. *See* RUAA § 17(e) ((e). (An arbitrator may issue a protective order to prevent the disclosure of privileged information, confidential information, trade secrets, and other information protected from disclosure).

Privacy or confidentiality can be valuable to parties for a number of reasons, not least of which is that the parties may want to protect trade secrets or other intellectual property rights. But parties may also agree that their business just isn't everyone else's. Privacy or confidentiality can help reduce the strife in a dispute resolution process and keep parties from using the threat of bad press as a strategic advantage.

That said, as the #MeToo movement has demonstrated and as a raft of recent empirical evidence establishes, confidentiality often functions to isolate victims, shield serial predators from accountability, and allow harassment to persist in organizations. As a result, several states have pending laws that could limit the degree to which confidentiality might apply in arbitration, at least in some sorts of disputes.

E.   Pro: Assuring Standards of Decision

Parties may turn to arbitration for more substantive reasons. Because arbitrators are both empowered and bound by the authority vested in them by the parties, the parties can define what decisional standards arbitrators will use.   Ordinarily, arbitrators apply applicable substantive law to resolve disputes, but parties may alter this.

For example, parties might prefer decision makers apply customs or industry norms. Think back to the Xmas Walnut. My wife and her brother and their family have created their own web of norms and conventions about the right to place the ornament on the tree. A court applying law might wind up ignoring, overlooking, or simply under-valuing the importance of these norms. A decision maker empowered to understand and apply these norms could render a decision more in line with the parties' actual experience and expectations.

In the context of international disputes, parties may want arbitrators to apply anational or transnational rules of decision instead of otherwise applicable national law. One of the advantages to international commercial arbitration, in fact, can be that arbitrators rely on a more harmonized set of norms and expectations governing international businesses than the law of any particular jurisdiction would provide. Sometimes, parties might even prefer that their dispute be resolved by decision makers applying trade or industry norms or general principles of equity instead of legal rules. The key point is that in arbitration, unlike public courts, the parties can select, at least to some degree, the substantive decisional standards that adjudicators will apply.

F. Pro: International Benefits

Internationally, arbitration constitutes the key mechanism for adjudicating disputes. Parties to cross-border transactions opt for arbitration over judicial litigation for at least two important reasons (beyond the one mentioned in the previous section).

First, arbitration provides a neutral forum, allowing parties to avoid worries about "hometown" or "homecourt" advantage— concerns about litigating in the other party's national courts. Not only is the concern that the home courts of one party might be biased in that party's favor, but that party will have more ready access to attorneys who are experienced in litigating in those courts.

Second, and perhaps more importantly, parties agree to arbitrate because the Convention on the Recognition and Enforcement of Foreign Arbitral Awards (the New York Convention) makes it easier to enforce arbitral awards than court judgments in foreign jurisdictions. The New York Convention obligates contracting countries to enforce international arbitral awards obtained in another signatory country on a nondiscriminatory basis and with only a modicum of judicial supervision. Chapter 9 will address the Convention in more detail, but in essence, it allows a winner in arbitration to take the award to any court in any signatory country and have the award enforced. No analogue to the New York Convention exists for the cross-border enforcement of public court judgments.

G. Pro: Class Action Waiver (Well, a Pro for Businesses, at Least)

Especially in the context of business-to-consumer or employment contracts, one of the primary reasons a business party might choose arbitration is to avoid aggregative dispute resolution, like class actions.

Class actions, as you probably know, allow parties (usually plaintiffs) to band together. Aggregative dispute resolution can be efficient, because it allows similar claims and defenses by different parties to be handled collectively. But the real importance of class actions is that they allow plaintiffs with small-value harms to pool resources and damages. Imagine Belinda Bank Customer who alleges that Big Bank has improperly taken a $1 fee from her checking account every month for the past two years. If she's right, Belinda has suffered a harm, but it makes no sense for her to sue Big Bank over $24. Chances are, though, if this happened to Belinda it has happened to other customers of Big Bank. If Belinda can find 100,000 customers who have suffered the same harm, their total losses are $2,400,000. If these harmed individuals can combine their losses, that's plenty of money to make it worth fighting about!

A large body of literature explores the benefits and limitations of class actions, and not surprisingly, opinions about it vary greatly. What's certain, however, is that class actions expose businesses to significant liability. So, businesses began including arbitration provisions in their contracts with consumers and employees and then added, as part of those provisions, a clause that waived the right to pursue claims collectively.

According to the Supreme Court of the United States, these so-called "class action waivers" are perfectly consistent with arbitration law. In a series cases, the Supreme Court has systematically confirmed that class action waivers contained in arbitration agreements are enforceable.

We'll talk more about some these cases and the issue of class action waivers in Chapter 8. But the big thing to see for now is that stronger parties may include such waivers and thereby substantially limit the litigation leverage created by aggregative processes.

2. Some Cons

Some parties might think of several of the "advantages" discussed in the previous sections as "disadvantages." For instance, the availability of class action waivers in arbitration may constitute a significant disadvantage for some parties who are unable to efficiently and effectively vindicate rights absent aggregative process. Similarly, some parties might prefer to bring into public light certain classes of disputes, both as a strategic matter and as a matter of fundamental or perceived justice.

Beyond these disadvantages, arbitration poses several systematic potential disadvantages.

A. Con: Lack of Error Correction in High-Stakes Cases (No Appeals)

Arbitration can be a risky business. The lack of judicial oversight sometimes leaves parties feeling vulnerable to excessive or flatly wrong judgments. In "bet the farm" cases, or in cases involving novel rights, parties might crave the safety of a second set of eyes reviewing their awards. Because arbitration does not have any appeals process, and because arbitration law severely circumscribes the judicial review of arbitral awards, the fear of an aberrational award may make public court litigation more attractive.

Importantly, to help offset this disadvantage, more recently, a number of arbitration institutions have created optional appellate procedures. These procedures, however, are relatively new and remain largely untested.

B. Con: Risk of Split-the-Difference Awards (Maybe?)

Arbitrators may have incentives to avoid rendering too decisive a victory to any party. A losing party may hold a grudge against an arbitrator. That losing party might then refuse to appoint the arbitrator in another case or might sully the arbitrator's reputation. To avoid these possibilities, arbitrators might be inclined towards a compromise, "split the difference" award, reminiscent of King Solomon's famous threat to cut a baby in two. [2]

Notably, the empirical evidence, while limited, does not seem to support this worry. To the contrary, what evidence we have suggests that arbitrators take their adjudicative role as seriously as judges. But parties might still worry about this risk and prefer to avoid arbitration because of it.

C. Con: Higher Up-Front Costs

Arbitration usually has higher up-front costs than public court litigation. Parties are paying, at the least, for the arbitrators and often for administrative services of an institution. Arbitration filing and administrative fees can be as high as thousands of dollars per case, and the hourly rates for arbitrators may range between $250 to $1500 (or more). So, arbitration can be extremely expensive,

---

[2] I never know whether to include this reference because it sort of misses the point of the Biblical story, I think. I'm no Biblical scholar, but I believe King Solomon was faced, in the story, with a custody dispute and was making the baby-cutting threat as a ploy to discover the true mother. The true mother, the logic went, would never let the baby be hacked in two. Still, the reference is common in writings about possible drawbacks to arbitration, so I'll include it here.

particularly in more complicated cases, at least at the outset. Plaintiffs generally are expected to cover half of these costs.

Importantly, as we'll discuss in Chapter 8, this concern may be mitigated in the context of consumer, employee, and weaker party arbitrations, at least to some extent, by stronger parties agreeing or being forced to bear the brunt of these higher up-front costs. At least sometimes, arbitration may be significantly cheaper for individuals, as stronger parties may pay all of the weaker parties' costs.

D. Con: Lower Damages Awards (Maybe?)

A general perception exists that arbitrators give smaller awards than juries. It's not clear that's true. Limited empirical evidence exists, and what evidence there is may not tell the whole story. For instance, because arbitrations may be cheaper for individuals, as discussed in the previous section, and thus easier to pursue, more questionable claims might be asserted in arbitration than would be in public court. The greater percentage of weak claims in arbitration may depress average arbitration awards.

In any event, whatever the empirical reality, corporate defendants certainly seem to believe that they are likely to get more sympathy from arbitrators, if not downright bias in their favor. On the flip side, plaintiffs' attorneys certainly seem to believe that their clients may wind up with less recovery in arbitration. These beliefs shape choices about when and why parties choose or resist arbitration.

E. Con: Repeat Player Problems with Arbitrators (Possibly but . . .)

Arbitrators know who butters their bread. That's the idea behind the repeat player worry.

There may be an asymmetry in how often parties find themselves in arbitration. An individual may only have one arbitration in her entire life. In contrast, a large company will probably have numerous arbitrations in a given year. Because arbitrators get paid only when they are working on a case, they have an economic stake in being selected for multiple appointments. Accordingly, their judgment may be shaded by a desire to build a "track record" of decisions that corporate repeat-users will like. Unsurprisingly, at least one study has detected that corporate defendants have a repeat-player advantage in arbitration.

That said, arbitral institutions have taken steps to offset this possible repeat-player bias, putting internal limits on how many times an individual arbitrator may be appointed in cases involving the same corporate defendants in consumer and employment cases. Additionally, arbitration law requires that arbitrators be "impartial." At least in theory, this limitation should prevent or impede the most egregious instances of repeat player bias.

CHAPTER 3

Five Core Concepts at the Heart of Arbitration

Finding simplicity out of clutter requires seeing the big picture. That's the goal of this Chapter.

A handful of concepts and doctrines form the core of arbitration law. The relationships between these concepts and doctrines as well as the individual details can be complex. But this Chapter gives you a concise primer that should help you see the forest of arbitration law and practice from 10,000 feet.

1. Freedom of Contract (and Its Limits)

You already know that arbitration amounts to a choice and a commitment: the choice to opt out of the public court system and commit instead to having a dispute adjudicated in arbitration. Put more simply, arbitration distills to a matter of contract.

As the U.S. Supreme Court said in *Volt Info. Scis., Inc. v. Bd. of Trs. of Leland Stanford Junior Univ.*, 489 U.S. 468, 479 (1989):

[T]he FAA's primary purpose [is to] ensur[e] that private agreements to arbitrate are enforced according to their terms. Arbitration under the [FAA] is a matter of consent, not coercion, and parties are generally free to structure their arbitration agreements as they see fit. . . . By permitting the courts to "rigorously enforce" such agreements according to their terms, we give effect to the contractual rights and expectations of the parties.

This freedom of contract means that parties may devise ways to resolve their disputes however they want, suited to their needs and temperaments. They can do so even if the adjudicatory framework they come up with bears little resemblance to processes that might be used in a public court.

But just how free are parties? Are there any limits?

Sure, there are!

There just aren't many. Let's focus on three:

- **General contract law limits**—The parties must abide by the requirements of general contract law.

- **Procedural due process limits**—Whatever process the parties come up with, it must meet minimal requirements of procedural due process.

- **Functus officio limits**—The parties' power to shape the process of arbitration ends when the arbitrator issues a final award.

A. General Contract Law Limits

A consequence of arbitration agreements being regular ol' contracts is that they must be free from standard formation and enforcement defects. The arbitral clause must be the product of mutual assent and it must be supported by consideration. Moreover, no generally applicable contract defenses or excuses for non-performance must apply—there must be no duress, no fraud, no unconscionability, mutual mistake, and so forth.

B. *Procedural Due Process Limits*

The adjudicatory system the parties come up with won't be recognized as an alternative to public courts if it doesn't meet the minimal requirements of procedural due process.

Unfortunately, there can be quite a bit of debate about what constitutes minimal standards of procedural due process. It's probably not fair to say that due process is in the eye of the beholder, but it may be fair to say that it's like the definition of obscenity—you know it when you see it.

As a result, a full exploration of exactly what procedural due process means or requires would not be short or happy. Philosophers, courts, lawyers, professors, and legislators have provided various framings of the concept both domestically and internationally for hundreds of years.

Still, whatever description one prefers, the concept is omnipresent. Almost every constitution of a democratic country carries the idea of due process, and the doctrine has also found its way into international conventions and treaties such as Universal Declaration of Human Rights. No one doubts the relevance and importance of procedural due process. So, we also can't ignore it.

For our purposes, it's maybe enough to simplify quite a bit. I think about it by starting with the Red Queen, who declared, "Sentence first, verdict afterwards!"[1] The trouble with this, of course, is that prejudging the outcome of a case and always ruling against one party—the accused in the Red Queen's proclamation—

---

[1] LEWIS CARROL, ALICE'S ADVENTURES IN WONDERLAND (1865), *reprinted in* THE ANNOTATED ALICE 161 (Martin Gardner ed., 1960).

without any consideration of the merits can't amount to a procedurally sufficient process.

From here, I turn to a hypothetical: imagine a decision maker resolving a dispute by flipping a coin or studying the entrails of a dead bird. Would relying on such standards of decision count as legitimate? Considering why or why not can help us illuminate the minimal standards of due process.

Let's start with the coinflip. Rendering a decision based on a coin flip certainly isn't quite as bad as the Red Queen's prejudgment, which condemns one side to always lose. But it still doesn't have anything to do with the merits of the dispute. Rendering a decision based on a coin flip makes anything the parties could say about their respective positions irrelevant. Although we could label a coin toss resolution "fair" in the sense that there's no decision maker bias to worry about and the parties have an equal opportunity to prevail, the outcome does not depend, in any sense, on what actually occurred. Accordingly, a coin toss results in a purely random outcome.

Due process probably requires more. Equal treatment of the parties matters, as the Red Queen fails to appreciate, but the equality we generally seek in a dispute resolution process focuses on equality of an opportunity to be heard and have each side's arguments considered. It's not even that the outcome always needs to be accurate or correct. It's that the process leading to an outcome needs to give both sides a reasonably fair opportunity to be meaningful participants. A coin flip probably doesn't cut it.

One could object here that, if both parties agree to use the coinflip method as a way of conclusively ending strife between them, why shouldn't we let them? I'm not entirely convinced that we shouldn't. In fact, I was once involved in a settlement where that's precisely what the parties did to solve a small, lingering issue of contention. It worked quite nicely.

The trouble may arise when the parties enter into a pre-dispute stipulation to resolve a future fight through a coin toss. The parties don't know what the stakes are or what the facts will be. At that point, it's harder to imagine that any rational party would submit themselves to the happenstance of a coinflip. Still, at least between sophisticated parties who are actually negotiating for such a mechanism, maybe we shouldn't second guess their ability to protect their own interests?

Rendering a decision based on "reading" the dead entrails of a bird runs afoul of another procedural due process norm.[2] Specifically, there's no discernable standard of decision. Unless both parties have an extremely strong faith in divination, such a process gives the decision maker complete and unchecked discretion to do whatever she wants. Moreover, the decision maker could, under the guise of "reading" the entrails, hide potential bias.

Procedural due process demands better. The decision maker cannot rule on whim, though bounds of what this means leave plenty of room for parties to select a wide range of standards of decision. Ruling according to law, after all, is not the only way to rule in a principled fashion. Moreover, the decision maker must be unbiased—or the parties must accept the decision maker as unbiased, more precisely. Any standard of decision that allows a decision maker to conceal her bias will not work.

The bottom line is that parties have a lot of freedom to design their own processes, but some backstop of minimal procedural due process prevents parties from flouting that freedom.

---

[2] Sorry, I couldn't help the word play!

Doctrinally, the narrow grounds for judicial review of arbitral awards supposedly assure that minimal standards of due process exist. So, if you want to challenge a particular arbitration process as being violative of procedural due process norms, you probably need to squeeze your arguments into the review stage. In practice, the narrow grounds for review may or may not be sufficient, but courts can and do stretch these grounds to address remarkable departures from what they view as the requirements of procedural due process. It is also possible that a process, from the outset, could look so unfair as to create a basis for arguing that the arbitration clause is unconscionable or outright fraudulent.

C. *Functus Officio* Limits

At least in the United States, parties' power to shape the arbitral process terminates when the arbitration closes. That happens when the arbitrator issues a final award. At that point, the arbitration is *functus officio.*

In practical terms, this means that parties cannot alter the standards of judicial review of arbitral awards. Remember, once the arbitrator issues an award, a party might seek a court's assistance to either confirm the award or vacate it. The court will then review the award on narrow and limited grounds to decide what it should do. The review standards constitute both the floor and the ceiling of judicial authority, and that authority cannot be altered by the agreement of the parties.

2. Arbitrability

"Arbitrability" is a fancy word for jurisdiction. Arbitrability, in other words, constitutes an umbrella concept referring to the arbitrator's ability to hear a dispute.

The question of whether a dispute can be lawfully submitted to arbitration—whether a dispute is "arbitrable" or conversely "inarbitrable"—can be raised at three different times:

- Time 1—in a court at the outset as a defense to the enforcement of the arbitral agreement;

- Time 2—to the arbitrator as a justification for ending the arbitral process; or

- Time 3—in a court as a defense to the enforcement of the arbitral award.

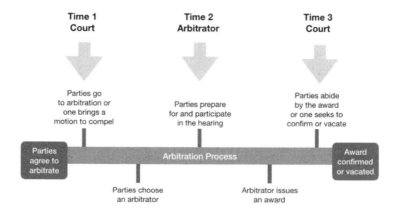

Although most case law does not use this taxonomy explicitly, we're going to distinguish between two forms of arbitrability:

- **Subject-matter arbitrability**—The federal congress could, in theory, place limits on what subjects are resolvable through arbitration.

- **Contractual arbitrability**—Because the parties' contract gives the arbitrator her authority, any flaws or limitations in that contract will prevent the arbitrator from having jurisdiction.

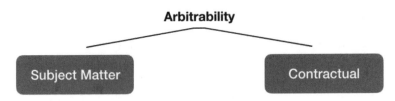

Arbitrability

Subject Matter   Contractual

A. *Subject Matter Arbitrability*

In theory, some subjects or topics could be excluded from the reach of arbitration on the basis of social policy concerns. For instance, a government might conclude that claims related to discrimination should not be arbitrable.

All sorts of reasons exist for a government to decide that some matters are not fit for resolution in arbitration. Governments could conclude that the arbitration of some categories of disputes would undermine citizens' perception of justice or fairness or remove from public view disputes implicating important public interests. Governments might decide that enforcement of some rights would be hampered without access to aggregative processes. Governments might conclude that certain domains need the accumulation of precedent generated by public courts.

Whatever the reason, almost all developed countries, particularly in Europe, place subject matter limitations on what can be arbitrated. In the EU, for instance, consumers and most employees cannot be forced to arbitrate claims against businesses in pre-dispute arbitration agreements.

The United States differs from the much of the rest of the world, however, and takes an extremely expansive view of arbitration and subject matter arbitrability. And when I say extremely expansive, I really mean it. Virtually every subject of civil law may be arbitrated.

Two points are critical.

First, the U.S. Supreme Court has made it clear that states cannot impede the recourse to arbitration on public policy grounds. In other words, states have absolutely no power to discriminate against arbitration contracts. State law—be it statutory, administrative, or case law—cannot prohibit or even obstruct arbitration. As discussed in Chapter 4, the FAA § 2 preempts any such efforts. So, states have no power to decide that certain subjects are inarbitrable and thus no role to play in regulating recourse to arbitration.

Second, that leaves the Federal Congress with sole authority to declare certain subjects inarbitrable. To date, however, only a handful of federal statutes limit the arbitrability of claims arising under them. Instead, almost all claims arising under statutes promoting significant social interests have been found to be arbitrable. These include claims under the antitrust laws, securities laws, Title VII, the Americans with Disabilities Act, the Employee Retirement Income Securities Act, the Truth-in-Lending Act, and the Magnuson-Moss Warranty Act.

Nevertheless, it's worth recognizing, that in recent years there has been growing interest in resurrecting at least some form of subject matter inarbitrability. Versions of an "Arbitration Fairness Act" have been bandied around Washington in the past two decades. Although few efforts have resulted in any passed legislation, limited exceptions do exist.

In 2002, for instance, President Bush signed into law a bill making pre-dispute arbitration clauses unenforceable in motor vehicle franchise agreements—contracts governing the business relationship between car dealers and car manufacturers. *See* Motor Vehicle Franchise Contract Arbitration Fairness Act, 15 U.S.C. § 1226. The legislation does not address the use of arbitration clauses in contracts between car dealers and their customers (or car dealers and their employees).

More recently, in 2017, the Bureau of Consumer Financial Protection ("CFPB") issued a final rule regulating arbitration agreements in contracts for particular consumer financial products and services. It did so pursuant to authority granted to it under the Dodd-Frank Wall Street Reform and Consumer Protection Act. Among other things, the CFPB rule prohibited covered service providers from using arbitration agreements to bar consumers from filing or participating in class actions.

Whatever one thinks of its merits, the CFPB rule was quite short-lived. On Nov. 1, 2017, the President signed a joint resolution passed by Congress disapproving the Arbitration Agreements Rule under the Congressional Review Act. Still, the passage of the rule suggests that there may be constituencies who believe that some limits on what matters can be arbitrated need to exist. Politics being what they are, those constituencies may, at some point, be able to effect changes to what is subject matter arbitrable in the United States.

B. *Contractual Arbitrability*

A consequence of arbitration being a matter of contract is that if a problem exists with the contract or if the contract doesn't cover a particular dispute, the arbitrator has no power. Similarly, if there's an unsatisfied procedural precondition to the obligation to arbitrate, the arbitrator has no power.

Put more directly, there are three questions that we need to ask:

- **Are there flaws in the agreement?** Does a valid and enforceable contract to arbitrate exist?

- **Does the dispute fall within the scope of the agreement?** Assuming that a valid arbitration contract exists, did the parties commit to arbitrate the specific dispute at issue?

- **Are there any preconditions to the right to arbitrate?** Assuming that a valid arbitration contract exists, are there any conditions to the right to arbitrate that have not been satisfied?

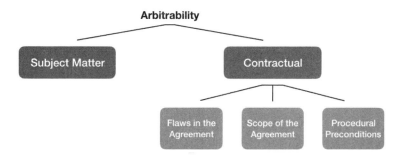

i. Flaws in the Arbitration Agreement

The first subcategory—flaws in the agreement—focuses whether a valid arbitration contract exists. Arbitration contracts may be unenforceable for any of the generally applicable grounds for refusing to recognize or enforce any contract, such as a lack of consideration or lack of mutual assent or the presence of fraud, duress, undue influence, unconscionability, or the like.

So, for instance, imagine that Alejo and Tueller enter into a contract to sell Alejo's car. Alejo drafts an arbitration agreement on a separate piece of paper. The arbitration agreement commits both parties to resolve their disputes in arbitration. Alejo, however, labels the arbitration agreement a "personal guarantee" and tells Tueller that it simply says that if Tueller doesn't pay as required by the sale agreement, Alejo can come after him personally for the money. Tueller knows Alejo and trusts him, so he doesn't actually read the document. He thinks a "personal guarantee" is silly and unnecessary, but he goes ahead and signs it. The car sale goes through, with both Alejo and Tueller performing, but a month later, Tueller discovers a problem. He sues Alejo in a public court. In response, Alejo produces the arbitration agreement and claims that the court should stay the litigation and compel Tueller to go to arbitration.

In this situation, Tueller will challenge the validity of the arbitration agreement on the basis of fraud. He did not understand that he was agreeing to arbitration. He was misled into believing, in fact, that he was signing a personal guarantee. Because he will challenge the validity of the arbitration contract using a generally applicable contract defense, before arbitration can occur, a decision maker must determine if Tueller really assented or whether fraud undermines arbitrability.

ii.   Scope of the Arbitration Agreement

The second subcategory—scope—evaluates whether the arbitration agreement's scope of application encompasses the particular dispute. Even if a valid contract for arbitration exists, parties might decide to exempt specific disputes or categories of disputes from arbitration. In other words, parties might carve out certain matters and reserve them for resolution in public courts.

The language of the arbitration clause determines the scope of what's arbitrable. The agreement to arbitrate, then, like any contract, must be interpreted to determine the scope of its application. The party opposing arbitration has the burden of proving that the dispute falls outside of the arbitration agreement's coverage.

Consider the car sale between Alejo and Tueller again. Let's imagine that as part of the sale, these parties also agree that Alejo will pay for car washes for one year. So, the contract has two components: sale of the car and provision of a service by Alejo related to the car. The arbitration agreement provides that "the parties shall arbitrate any and all disputes arising out of or related to the services portion of this contract. All other disputes may be resolved in a court of competent jurisdiction." A fight about the quality of the car arises. Tueller files a lawsuit against Alejo in a public court. Alejo wants to compel arbitration.

In this situation, Alejo should lose and Tueller's lawsuit should proceed. The parties' have only consented to have a subset of all possible disputes between them arbitrated, and the particular dispute that exists doesn't fall within that subset. Accordingly, there's no agreement to arbitrate this particular dispute.

iii. Preconditions to Arbitration

The third subcategory—preconditions—looks to see if the parties' promises to arbitrate are conditioned on the occurrence of certain events.

A condition, in contract law, amounts to an event not certain to occur, which must occur unless its nonoccurrence is excused, before performance of a promissory obligation becomes due. That's a pretty technical way of saying that conditions are sequencing devices telling us when performances under a contract are owed.

The nonsatisfaction of a condition means that, even if there's a valid arbitration agreement, the parties are not yet obligated to perform their promise to arbitrate. The time for their performance has not yet come.

Procedural preconditions to arbitration can take any number of forms, but a few common ones are:

- Limitations periods, such as requirements that claims be raised within a certain period (180 days, for instance);

- Requirements to participate in negotiation or mediation (or both) prior to filing an arbitration claim; and

- Notice requirements, such as requirements that complaints be made in writing and delivered to a particular address or party.

Procedural preconditions might also arise from the general context of the agreement. For instance, claims that one party has waived its right to proceed to arbitration or that arbitration is prevented by laches or estoppel could be considered failures of a precondition.

So, going back to Alejo and Tueller's car sale agreement, let's now imagine that the arbitration agreement commits them to resolve "any and all disputes by arbitration, but only after the parties have attempted, in good faith, to negotiate a resolution for at least 30 days." Let's assume that after the sale, a dispute arises and Tueller wants to file an arbitration claim against Alejo.

The arbitral clause in their contract means that Tueller cannot lawfully initiate arbitration unless and until he attempts to negotiate with Alejo over the dispute, in good faith, for 30 days. If he files the arbitration before that negotiation has occurred, the dispute will not be arbitrable.

3. Separability

Separability is easy to understand, but it may be harder to accept. Even seasoned lawyers sometimes have difficulty with the doctrine.

Separability means that arbitral clauses must be treated as analytically distinct from the container contracts in which they usually appear. Promises to arbitrate are independent and separate from whatever other substantive promises parties have made.

Easy, right? So, why's it such a big deal?

Well, separability has the potential to limit court supervision of the arbitral process. Specifically, the doctrine could mean that challenges based on a flaw in the arbitration agreement cannot, in practice, be made at Time 1—to a court as a defense to enforcement of the arbitration agreement.

An example might help.

Imagine Prima Paint Co. enters into an agreement with a competitor, the F&C Company, to buy all of F&C's paint business. During the acquisition, F&C makes a number of representations to Prima Paint about the business and assets. Shortly after this acquisition deal is signed, the parties enter into a second contract whereby F&C will provide consulting services to Prima Paint related to the business for a period of several years in exchange for a consulting fee. A year later, when the first installment of the consulting fee comes due, Prima Paint refuses to pay, saying that it was fraudulently induced into buying F&C's business and thus into the consulting agreement. It says that F&C misrepresented that it was solvent when, in fact, it was not.

The consulting agreement contains a broadly worded arbitration provision, saying that "any controversy or claim arising out of or relating to this agreement shall be settled by arbitration." F&C argues that, pursuant to this provision, Prima Paint must arbitrate any dispute including the fraudulent inducement claim. Prima Paint, on the other hand, says that the whole agreement, including the arbitration clause, was induced by fraud and therefore is not enforceable. What should the court do?

The court should send the matter to arbitration![3]

That result might not sit well with you. After all, if Prima Paint is right, then there was no contract at all. Fraud would make the contract voidable. And if there was no contract for the consulting services, then there would be no need to have an arbitration clause, so that clause shouldn't or doesn't exist.

But that's where separability comes into play.

The doctrine of separability requires that the court pull the arbitration clause out and treat it as separate and independent from the container contract. Although Prima Paint alleged that it was fraudulently induced into entering into the container contract and its substantive obligations, it has not claimed that it was fraudulently induced into agreeing that disputes arising out of or related to that container agreement would be arbitrated. Because Prima Paint was not deceived into promising to arbitrate, it has to fight about the validity of the container contract in arbitration.

Think of it this way: Is the claim that the container contract was induced by fraud a claim "arising out of or related to" the container contract? Of course it is! Did Prima Paint agree to arbitrate any such claims? Yeah, certainly. So, Prima Paint should have to do what it promised to do and go to arbitration.

Notice how this is different than hypothetical that appeared back in the section on contract arbitrability. Back in that section, Tueller was claiming that the arbitration agreement itself was induced by fraud—Alejo had told Tueller that the paper he was signing was a "personal guarantee" and not an arbitration agreement. Even if, instead of being a separate piece of paper, the arbitration agreement had appeared in a clause called

---

[3]   This is a simplified version of what happened in the leading U.S. Supreme Court case *Prima Paint Corp. v. Flood & Conklin Mfg. Co.*, 388 U.S. 395 (1967).

"personal guarantee" in the container contract, the separability doctrine would not apply. A court would presumptively get to decide the issue of whether fraud existed and undermined the arbitrability of the dispute.

The doctrine of separability establishes that unless a party specifically challenges the validity of arbitration clause itself—as opposed to the container contract—the dispute remains arbitrable. Allegations of contractual invalidity made against the container contract do not necessarily taint the arbitral clause. The challenging party must establish that the alleged invalidity bears directly upon the arbitral clause. Otherwise, the reference to arbitration remains in effect, and the arbitral tribunal gets rule on whether there is a flaw in the container contract that undermines its validity.

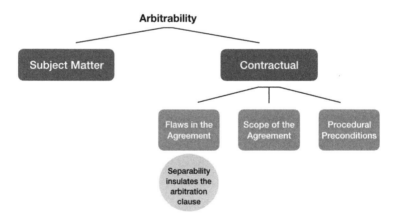

This last point is important. Separability does not mean that Prima Paint loses all opportunity to have its fraud claim heard. The doctrine instead allocates decision making authority over the claim to the arbitrator. A court at Time 1—when the enforceability of the arbitration agreement is challenged before the court—does not hear Prima Paint's fraud arguments. Instead, the court should send the matter to arbitration, and the arbitrator at Time 2 will decide if fraud in the inducement exists.

The doctrine of separability works in conjunction with the doctrine of kompentenz-kompentenz to protect the jurisdictional authority of arbitral tribunals and the autonomy of the arbitral process.

4. Kompentenz-Kompentenz

The concept of kompentenz-kompentenz,[4] also known as jurisdiction to rule on jurisdictional challenges, provides that the arbitral tribunal has the authority to decide on its own authority. As we saw in earlier, "jurisdiction" in arbitration means "arbitrability." So, kompentenz-kompentenz basically means that arbitrators get to decide if there's arbitrability, or at least contractual arbitrability.

> *U.S. Courts rarely think about subject matter arbitrability because there are so few subject matter limits on what is arbitrable. Accordingly, it's not entirely clear what decision maker decides whether subject matter arbitrability exists. It's a fair bet to guess that courts should always decide this question, and that would be consistent with international norms.*

While the term kompentenz-kompentenz may be new, the idea should be familiar to you, if you have any background in public court procedure. Public courts must have both personal and subject matter jurisdiction in order to rule on the merits of a case. If a court lacks these forms of jurisdiction, it does not have power. But what person or body decides if a court has jurisdiction? The court! Courts, in short, have jurisdiction to decide their own jurisdiction.

---

4   Kompentenz-kompenenz in German and compéntence-compéntence in French.

And, so do arbitrators. At least they do internationally. Most countries embrace this concept. The U.S. does as well, but in a somewhat roundabout way.

In the U.S., things are a little more complicated because courts presumptively have the authority to decide some sorts of contractual arbitrability. Specifically, courts have the obligation and power to resolve threshold questions about whether a valid arbitration agreement exists—when such questions are directed at the arbitration agreement specifically and not the container contract, as the doctrine of separability dictates—and questions about whether a dispute falls within the scope of an arbitration agreement.

In terms of the taxonomy of contract arbitrability introduced earlier, this means that courts have the obligation and power to decide questions (i) and (ii)—validity and scope.

This makes it sound like there is no such thing as kompentenz-kompentenz in the U.S. But that's not true for two reasons.

First, parties may delegate authority to arbitrators to decide questions (i) and (ii) in "clear and unmistakable" language in the arbitration clause. These delegations effectively give arbitrators the power to rule on their own jurisdiction and thus allow parties to opt into the concept of kompentenz-kompentenz.

The delegations that parties include to opt into kompentenz-kompentenz are occasionally referred to as *Kaplan* Delegation clauses after the U.S. Supreme Court case recognizing that parties have this power, *First Options of Chicago, Inc. v. Kaplan*, 514 U.S. 938, 944 (1995).

Second, under U.S. law, arbitrators always have jurisdiction to decide whether preconditions to arbitration have been satisfied. In terms of the taxonomy of contract arbitrability discussed earlier, this means that arbitrators always decide question (iii)—preconditions.

Like separability, kompentenz-kompentenz functions to insulate and protect the arbitral process. Arbitrators need to be able to decide whether they have jurisdiction or else the feeblest challenge could abort the proceedings, and parties to legitimate arbitration agreements would be thrown into courts contrary to their bargain.

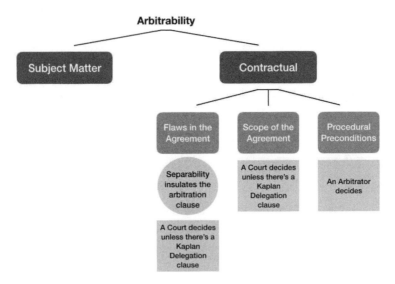

5. Limited Judicial Involvement and Review

As all four previous concepts and doctrines suggest, courts have an extremely limited role to play in arbitration. Arbitration law and practice exist to validate and enforce the parties' choice to commit themselves to arbitration. If they have made that choice and commitment, courts need to get out of the way and respect the arbitral process.

Mostly.

Courts do play a couple of roles, however.

First, courts have a supervisory role to play. This role means that courts:

- (1) assure that a valid arbitration agreement exists;

- (2) compel parties to abide by the terms of such an agreement;

- (3) review the arbitral process to make sure that it comports with minimal standards of procedural due process;

- (4) correct minor typographical or calculation errors in an award that do not impact the substance of the award; and

- (5) provide a mechanism for translating arbitral awards into court judgments that allow for enforcement through court processes.

We've already spent some time talking about (1) and (2), though Chapter 7 will examine these matters in greater detail.

Issues (3), (4), and (5) involve what's customarily called review and enforcement of arbitral awards. Chapter 8 will examine these matters more closely, but it's important to note now that judicial review of arbitral awards does not permit any reevaluation by a court of the merits of the dispute. There are, in short, no appeals from a wrongly decided arbitral decision.

Second, courts have a role to play in aiding the arbitral process. For instance, arbitration laws provide ways for courts to lend some of their powers to arbitrators to help with evidence gathering (issuing subpoenas to third party witnesses, for instance) and providing interim relief (injunctions) to maintain the status quo between the parties.

CHAPTER 4

Arbitration Laws
and Federalism

Think of the Federal Arbitration Act ("FAA") as the royal flush of statutes.

There are state statute analogues to the FAA, and those have some residual role to play in arbitration law and practice. But at this point in history, the U.S. Supreme Court has rewritten the FAA so that it applies broadly, preempts any inconsistent state laws, and forms a national and harmonious body of arbitration law. I often tell my students that the Supreme Court has made the right to go to arbitration a fundamental civil right, on par with other fundamental rights like freedom of speech or the right to assemble. The FAA's preemptive force combined with its extensive range of application means that state law often takes a backseat (or gets left at the curbside).

As you consider the FAA, note that the Supreme Court's pliant reading of the Act may be functional, but it is not necessarily analytically coherent. Ultimately, the Supreme Court's interpretation of the FAA matters a lot more than the actual text, which is barebones at best. Additionally, ample historic evidence indicates that the FAA was originally passed with modest procedural aspirations, designed to foster and protect commercial arbitration in federal courts. The reading that the U.S. Supreme Court has given to the Act, which expands it to be an all-purpose, federal law promoting arbitration between all sorts of parties nationwide, cannot be comfortably squared with either the text of the Act or its history.

This Chapter starts by giving you an overview of the functions performed by arbitration laws generally. It then turns to a brief tour of the key sections of the FAA before summarizing the ascendency of the Act to become the supreme arbitration law of the United States. The Chapter ends by considering a few features and functions of state arbitration laws, focusing primarily on the Revised Uniform Arbitration Act ("RUAA"), which has been adopted by 23 states as of 2018 and represents an example of a modern arbitration statute.

1. The Various Roles of Arbitration Laws

Party autonomy sits at the heart of arbitration. Seeing the relationship between the parties' contract and the law of arbitration can be tricky.

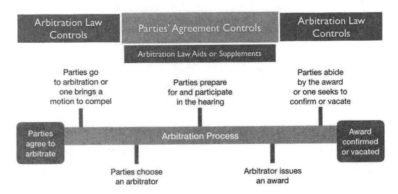

Arbitration law bookends the arbitral process, providing mandatory rules that:

- **Place any public policy limitations on what subjects can be arbitrated on the front end.** Arbitration laws (or laws regulating arbitration) may place limits on what subjects are arbitrable. In the United States, as you've seen, there are almost no such limits, and if any future limits were to be imposed, they would have to come from the federal Congress.

- **Validate and enforce the parties' agreement to arbitrate on the front end.** Perhaps the most fundamental function of modern arbitration laws is to reverse the old judicial hostility to arbitration and make arbitration agreements enforceable to the same extent as any other contracts. If a valid, written agreement to arbitrate a particular dispute exists, then arbitration laws establish that courts should enforce those agreements by forcing parties to do what they promised and go to arbitration. This means that arbitration laws provide for the remedies of a stay on any pending public court litigation and the right to compel a recalcitrant party to go to arbitration.

- **Establish mechanisms for judicial review and enforcement of arbitral awards on the backend.** Arbitration laws also establish the process by which public courts review and enforce arbitral awards. The review and enforcement process must be narrowly focused on evaluation of the arbitral process and not the merits so that judicial involvement does not become a sort of appellate review.

During the arbitration, arbitral law may:

- **Provide authority for courts to support or aid the arbitral process.** Arbitration laws provide various mechanisms allowing public courts to provide support or aid to the arbitral process. For instance, arbitration laws may permit courts to lend their subpoena powers to arbitrators or allow courts to enter injunctive relief without taking over the case.

- **Provide a menu of default rules that apply if parties do not opt out of them.** Many arbitration laws include default rules that apply if the parties don't opt out of them. For instance, if the parties opt to resolve future disputes by arbitration but fail to decide how many arbitrators there will be, arbitration laws provide a default—usually one arbitrator. Similarly, if parties fail to provide a mechanism for appointing arbitrators, arbitration laws usually provide that the default rule is that parties must agree to the appointment and, if they cannot, a public court will make the appointment for them.

The first three categories apply regardless of what the parties agree. Rules governing whether an arbitration agreement exists must be mandatory. These rules establish what counts as a valid and enforceable arbitration agreement, so it would put the cart before the horse to allow party autonomy to alter or change these rules. Similarly, the rules governing what subjects are arbitrable and review and enforcement of arbitral awards must be mandatory. These rules serve as the primary opportunity for public courts to assure that minimal standards of adjudicatory fairness are satisfied in the arbitral process.

The second two categories are not mandatory. These functions exist to help parties and arbitrators, but parties have the power to opt out of or alter or vary the law regarding these matters.

The last category in particular—default rules—is worth focusing on for a moment. That terminology may not be familiar to you.

When people think of law, they tend to think that law creates immutable directives that must be obeyed. Some laws do just that. Most criminal laws, for instance, or tort rules are mandatory. But not all legal directives are obligatory. Many rules are what may be called "default" rules. Such rules supply understandings that govern unless and until parties change them.

I think of it like this: when you buy a new smartphone, you can open up the box, turn the thing on, and start using it. You need to do very little to make the phone work. If you don't pick a ringtone, will the phone still ring if someone calls you? Of course! There's a ringtone set as a default. If you don't download a camera app, can you still take a selfie? Of course! There's a built-in camera application. But, you can change the ringtone and even add all sorts of very idiosyncratic ones, if you're so inclined. And you can add all sorts of applications to create the perfect picture. The phone, in short, has a lot of default settings that allow you to use it without doing anything. But you can also customize most of these settings to better meet your needs and preferences.

Many arbitration laws work similarly, allowing parties to opt out or customize them. These laws merely foster party autonomy, helping the parties who either don't think of everything or decide that trying to think of everything would be too much of a hassle or cost.

Most of the FAA addresses the bookends—most of the FAA rules, in other words, are mandatory. State law, on the other hand, primarily aids and supplements the arbitral process.

2. A Brief Tour of the FAA

Enacted in 1925, the FAA sets the legislative framework for the enforcement of arbitration agreements and arbitral awards in the United States. Because the gloss put on the Act by the U.S. Supreme Court matters so much, this tour will highlight what the most significant provisions of the Act have been read to mean rather than what they say.

A. Section 1 of the FAA: Scope of the Act

FAA § 1 defines when the federal law of arbitration applies, and it applies to pretty much everything.

Specifically, the FAA applies to arbitration agreements in:

- **Maritime transactions**, meaning any transactions taking place on navigable waterways.

- **Transactions involving Interstate Commerce**, meaning any transaction that affects interstate commerce.

Maritime law matters a lot in the real world of commerce, but for our purposes, it's enough to say simply that the definition of what counts as a navigable waterway and thus what counts as a maritime transaction is expansive. I once had an admiralty law professor tell me that it would even be arguable that a rubber ducky floating in a child's bath would be on a navigable waterway! That might have been hyperbole, but if the transaction involves something on water, even if it's not on the "high seas," the transaction could be maritime in nature.

But the scope of maritime law rarely matters in arbitration practice because the U.S. Supreme Court's expansive reading of "involving commerce" sweeps in just about every imaginable transaction, on a navigable waterway or not. According to the Court, "involving commerce" constitutes the functional equivalent of the more familiar term "affecting commerce"—words of art that ordinarily signal the broadest permissible exercise of Congress' Commerce Clause power.[1] At its broadest, Congress' Commerce Clause power knows almost no bounds.

It's also worth noting that the apparent exclusion at the end of FAA § 1 of arbitration agreements in "contracts of employment of seamen, railroad employees, or any other class of workers engaged in foreign or interstate commerce" does not mean what it seems to mean. On its face, this provision seems to be pretty straightforward: employment agreements are not covered by the FAA. That straight forward reading, however, does not apply.

In its march to rewrite the text of the Act, the U.S. Supreme Court has said that this provision excludes FAA application only in contracts of employment for workers physically engaged in interstate transportation—the workers actually moving stuff.[2] Arbitration agreements in individual employment contracts of all other employees are covered by the FAA.[3]

The bottom line: the FAA applies to most economic transactions in our modern national (and global) economy. Because it applies to pretty much every transaction, the FAA effectively constitutes the primary national law of arbitration.

---

[1] *See, e.g., Citizens Bank v. Alafabco, Inc.*, 539 U.S. 32 (2003); *Allied-Bruce Terminix Cos. v. Dobson*, 513 U.S. 265 (1995).

[2] *Circuit City Stores, Inc. v. Adams*, 532 U.S. 105 (2001).

[3] Arbitration pursuant to a collective bargaining agreement is governed by § 301 of Labor Management Relations Act ("LMRA"), 29 U.S.C. § 185(a).

B. *Section 2 of the FAA: Heart of the Act*

FAA § 2 assures that arbitration contracts are valid and irrevocable unless a generally applicable contract law would invalidate them.

To be valid, an arbitration agreement must be:

- **In writing.** This formality has been softened so that courts now allow any "record"—any electronic means of storing and repeating a message—to qualify and allow multiple records to be combined together to satisfy the requirements of an agreement.

- **Satisfy the requirements of general contract law.** Arbitration agreements are just contracts, so they must meet the standard requirements of contracts. Another way of saying this is that arbitration agreements may be invalidated on the basis of any generally applicable contract law defense.

FAA § 2 constitutes the centerpiece of the Act. Accordingly, several important points need to be made about it.

First, it expressly counters the common law's historic hostility toward arbitration. It reverses federal and state court precedents that had made pre-dispute arbitration agreements unenforceable, and it puts arbitration agreements on equal footing with other types of contracts.

Second, the so-called "savings clause" of the section preserves a critical role for state law. The section says that arbitration agreements are valid "save upon such grounds as exist at law or in equity for the revocation of any contract." The "grounds" that could exist for the revocation of "any contract" are state law grounds. Contract law is state law. So, more precisely, the FAA says that arbitration agreements, as a matter of federal law, are valid and enforceable unless a generally applicable state contract law defense would prevent enforcement.

Third, that "generally applicable" language really matters. The state contract law grounds that can prevent enforcement of an arbitration agreement must apply to all contracts. In other words, state law cannot single out arbitration contracts for special scrutiny. States cannot create special rules aimed at undermining the strong federal policy favoring the enforceability of arbitration agreements.

Finally, as this discussion suggests, FAA § 2 preempts any inconsistent state law. Under the Supremacy Clause of the United States Constitution, federal law takes precedence over conflicting state law. As preemptive federal law, FAA § 2 is equally applicable in federal and state courts.

C. Sections 3 and 4 of the FAA: Remedies for Breach of Arbitration Contracts

FAA §§ 3 and 4 provide that, if a valid arbitration agreement exists, a court shall stay any pending litigation and compel the parties to go to arbitration, as they promised to do.

To stay litigation and compel the parties to go to arbitration, a court must:

- **Determine that the agreement to arbitration is valid.** This means that the court must decide that FAA § 2 is satisfied and the arbitration agreement meets the generally applicable requirements of contract law.

- **Determine that the dispute in question is covered by the arbitration agreement.** This means that the court must determine that the particular dispute falls within the scope of the arbitration agreement.

- **Determine that the party seeking to arbitrate is not in default.** The final clause in FAA § 3 says that the party moving to stay litigation must "not [be] in default in proceeding with . . . arbitration." This means that the party seeking to force the other into arbitration cannot be in breach of the arbitration agreement.

FAA §§ 3 and 4 are the teeth of the Act. They outline the legal effects of an arbitration agreement that is "valid, irrevocable, and enforceable" under FAA § 2. Basically, a valid arbitration agreement divests the court of the right to entertain the dispute, and it entitles one party to compel the other to do what it promised—arbitrate.

Note that both sections 3 and 4 use the word "shall": if a valid arbitration agreement exists, the court "shall" stay any pending litigation and it "shall" send the parties to arbitration. This means that there's no discretion for a federal court to deny these remedies, even if compelling arbitration would amount to an inefficient or piecemeal adjudication of a dispute.

Also, notice that both sections refer only to federal courts. This textual reality underscores the fact that the FAA was, in its original form, a procedural act that applied only in federal court. Those narrow procedural days, however, are long past. At this point in history, the FAA creates a federally preemptive right and thus applies in federal and state courts. Although FAA §§ 3 and 4 are not directly applicable in state court, state courts must provide for functionally equivalent remedies to vindicate the right provided in FAA § 2.

Technically, the Supreme Court has never squarely said that the spirit of FAA §§ 3 and 4 are preemptive, but most commentators and lower courts agree that states must provide effectively the same remedies as those provided by federal law. See, e.g., See Southland v. Keating, 465 U.S. 1, 24 (O'Connor, J., dissenting) ("[T]he Court reads [FAA] § 2 to require state courts to enforce § 2 rights using procedures that mimic those specified for federal courts by FAA §§ 3 and 4.").

D. Sections 5 and 7 of the FAA: Aids to the Arbitral Process

FAA §§ 5 and 7 have a unifying theme: federal courts can help out the arbitral process.

FAA § 5 allows a federal court to help if the arbitration agreement fails, for whatever reason, to provide a mechanism for appointing an arbitrator. As you know, parties have the power to appoint the arbitrator or choose whatever mechanism will be used to appoint an arbitrator. Imagine, however, that the parties provide that "Professor Henry Blair will serve as the sole arbitrator in any dispute that arises between us" and Blair is unavailable for the next two years because he's so busy with other matters. In such a case, the mechanism that the parties selected has failed.

That's where FAA § 5 steps in. It constitutes an important fallback option in cases where one side attempts to evade or slow arbitration proceedings by refusing to cooperate in selecting arbitrators or where an agreed method for appointing arbitrators fails for some other reason.

FAA § 7 permits arbitrators to borrow certain evidence-gathering powers from a federal court. Specifically, the section authorizes arbitrators to summon (or subpoena) nonparties to provide evidence in arbitral proceedings.

Without a provision like FAA § 7, arbitrators would have no power to compel evidence from non-parties. Of course, arbitrators have power over the parties. Arbitrators can sanction noncompliance with any evidence-gathering order by ruling for the other side partially or completely. But arbitrators are just regular citizens with no judicial powers. They have no authority over non-parties. Accordingly, without a provision like FAA § 7, arbitration would stall, at least when the dispute turns on evidence from outside sources.

E. Sections 9, 10, and 11: Limited Judicial Oversight

FAA §§ 9, 10, and 11 provide the mechanisms by which parties can ask a court to confirm, vacate, and modify arbitral awards.

FAA § 9 establishes that a party, within one year of the rendering of the award, may apply to a court for an order confirming the award. A party who secures an arbitral award and has it confirmed can turn the award into a court a judgment. That, in turn, provides access to the court's authority and processes for enforcement, including garnishing of wages, post-judgment discovery of assets, and so on.

According to § 9, the court must confirm the award unless the award "is vacated, modified or corrected as proscribed in sections 10 and 11."

FAA § 12 provides a different limitations period for vacating an award: a challenge to the award must be made "within three months after the award is filed or delivered."

FAA § 10 articulates the grounds upon which a federal district court with appropriate jurisdiction can refuse to confirm and enforce an arbitral award. The action, known as "vacatur" of the award, renders the award legally unenforceable.

This section provides the court with an opportunity to review the arbitral process and make sure it was minimally fair. It provides four narrow and limited grounds for review:

- **Where the award was procured by corruption, fraud or undue means.** This provision polices against wholesale procedural illegitimacy. In short, it allows a court to overturn an award when the arbitrator has been fraudulently misled, or when one party has used threats of violence or other forms of intimidation to extract a favorable decision from the arbitrator. As you can imagine, these forms of procedural deficiencies are exceedingly rare.

- **Where there was evident partiality or corruption in the arbitrators.** This provision protects against the appearance of bias in the arbitrators. This ground may be the most significant basis for vacating an arbitral award, and it will be discussed in some detail in Chapter 7. For now, it is enough to note that arbitrators must not be evidently partial. The requirement focuses not on the actual bias of arbitrators, but on the appearance of bias. Accordingly, the mechanism for avoiding the appearance of bias is disclosure—so long as arbitrators disclose potential conflicts of interest, many issues of evident partiality can be avoided.

- **Where the arbitrators failed to hear material evidence or otherwise prejudiced a party's reasonable opportunity to be heard.** This provision seems more expansive than it has been read by courts to be. At bottom, arbitrators must give parties a reasonable and reasonably equal opportunity to be heard. This opportunity need not be perfect. It also doesn't need to be equivalent or even similar to the opportunity that a party would get in a public court.

• **Where the arbitrators exceeded their powers.** The arbitration agreement establishes the authority of the arbitrators. If arbitrators act beyond or outside the scope of their mandate, they are doing so without power. This usually means that arbitrators have ruled on a matter not submitted to them or not covered by the arbitration agreement, though it could also mean that the arbitrators have provided a remedy that goes beyond the limits placed on their authority. This ground can also be applicable if the arbitrators fail to do their jobs in some other respect.

FAA § 10 constitutes both the floor and the ceiling of judicial review of arbitral awards. In other words, if a party seeks to confirm or vacate an award, a federal court must review the award on these four grounds, and only these four grounds. (As you'll learn in Chapter 7, there may be one additional ground that courts can use to review awards, manifest disregard of the law. But you should note for now that this ground does not expressly appear in FAA § 10.)

Finally, be sure to see that none of these grounds permits a court to engage in any merits review of the award. To the contrary, these grounds focus only on procedural issues. *There is no judicial review of mistakes of law or fact by arbitrators.*

FAA § 11 allows for the enforcement of awards that contain minor, non-substantive errors. Under this section, federal courts, on the request of one of the parties, have the power to modify or correct awards for inadvertent technical errors like spelling mistakes, typos, or calculation errors. The errors in question must be "evident" and unrelated to any reconsideration of the merits.

F. Section 16 of the FAA: Appeals

FAA § 16 establishes the right of a party losing a motion to compel arbitration in a federal court to appeal that decision immediately. On the other hand, a party who has been compelled to arbitration cannot appeal that decision immediately.

This differential treatment obviously favors arbitration. Thematically, this section confirms that any doubts about the arbitrability of a dispute should be resolved in favor of arbitration.

3. What the FAA---?!? Federal Preemption

At this point in history, it's safe to say that the U.S. Supreme Court loves arbitration. It has magnified the importance of arbitration in a series of more than fifty cases in the past fifty years, making federal law preemptive, eliminating states' ability to regulate the recourse to arbitration, and making virtually all civil disputes arbitrable.

There are two very general branches to the story of Supreme Court's love affair with arbitration: a branch that charts the rise of federal preemption and a branch that charts the demise of any subject matter limitations on what can be arbitrated. These two branches sometimes intertwine or overlap, and they are related by the overall theme of growing affection for arbitration.

We're going to focus, here, on the federal preemption branch. You already know the outcome of the subject matter arbitrability branch—there are almost no subjects of civil law that are inarbitrable and states have no power to regulate what subjects are arbitrable.

With respect to the preemption story, we're going to fast-forward through it. It's not that the details are uninteresting or unimportant, but the goal here is help you see the major turning points of the tale.

The story starts when the Supreme Court was not so fond of arbitration. Lingering distrust of the arbitral process continued even after enactment of the FAA in 1925. For many years, the FAA was used primarily to enforce arbitration of business-to-business disputes. After World War II, arbitration became an increasingly popular method of resolving labor disputes, an arena for which Congress had developed a specified framework for arbitration to prevent violence and the resultant disruption of business. But the Supreme Court remained highly skeptical of arbitration in other situations.

Two cases, in particular, are worth mentioning: *Wilko v. Swan* and *Bernhardt v. Polygraphic Co. of America*. [4] These cases were decided within three years of one another—1953 and 1956, respectively—and they share a healthy dose of doubt about the propriety of arbitration.

In both cases, a majority of the Court reasoned that arbitration lacked critical due process protections: right to a jury trial where such would be available in a public court, reasoned opinions, judges trained in the law, fully-developed evidentiary standards, formal rights to discovery, and appellate review, among other things. According to the Court in *Bernhardt*, these limitations could substantially impact the outcome of disputes. While the Court in both cases also grudgingly recognized that arbitration had a role to play in the adjudication of some commercial disputes, the clear message of the cases was that arbitration needed to stay in its narrow lane.

---

[4] *Wilko v. Swan*, 346 U.S. 427 (1953), overruled by *Rodriguez de Quijas v. Shearson/Am. Exp., Inc.*, 490 U.S. 477 (1989); *Bernhardt v. Polygraphic Co. of Am., Inc.*, 350 U.S. 198 (1956).

That sentiment wouldn't really change until 1967, with the Court's decision in *Prima Paint v. Flood & Conklin Manufacturing Co.*[5] Substantively, *Prima Paint* ushered into U.S. arbitration law the doctrine of separability. But thematically, the case also ushered in a new era in how the Court would, for the next fifty years and counting, view arbitration more broadly. Although the *Prima Paint* Court stopped short of finding that the FAA created a federal substantive right to arbitrate, it set the stage for that eventual holding by concluding that the FAA was enacted pursuant to Congress's Commerce Clause power.

In a pair of key decisions in 1983 and 1984, the Court took the final step towards creating a preemptive federal law of arbitration. *Moses H. Cone Memorial Hosp. v. Mercury Construction. Corp.* and *Southland Corp. v Keating* confirmed that the FAA was intended to overcome the old judicial hostility toward arbitration.[6] Instead, the FAA represented a "congressional declaration of a liberal policy favoring arbitration agreements, notwithstanding any state substantive or procedural policies to the contrary." In other words, the FAA "create[s] a body of federal substantive law of arbitrability" equally applicable in both state and federal courts. According to the Court in *Southland*, this conclusion followed from the fact that Congress, by basing the FAA on its power "to enact substantive rules under the Commerce Clause," must have intended to make substantive law, binding on state as well as federal courts.

"[A]s a matter of federal law, *any* doubts concerning the scope of arbitrable issues should be resolved in favor of arbitration." The shorthand phrase that has been repeated literally thousands and thousands of times in lower court decisions and briefs for decades

---

[5]   388 U.S. 395 (1967).

[6]   *Southland Corp. v. Keating*, 465 U.S. 1 (1984); *Moses H. Cone Mem'l Hosp. v Mercury Constr. Corp.*, 460 U.S. 1 (1983).

is that the FAA created an emphatic "national policy favoring arbitration."

Since these cases, the Court has never looked back.

The conclusion that the FAA preempts state laws and applies equally in federal and state courts has been incredibly controversial, subject to strong criticisms by many U.S. Supreme Court Justices, lower court judges, and commentators. Despite this criticism, however, the Supreme Court has reaffirmed and repeatedly applied the holding in Southland.

There are at least four important things to note about the preemptive force of the FAA:

- **First, the FAA does not occupy the field of arbitration law.**

   Although it may be tempting, based on reading U.S. Supreme Court cases, to think that the FAA occupies the field of arbitration law, it does not. Instead, principles of conflict preemption govern the extent to which the FAA preempts state laws. This means that state arbitration laws—statutory and common law—are preempted if they actually conflict with federal law. The Supreme Court has explained that conflicts can arise when state law "stands as an obstacle to the accomplishment and execution of the full purposes and objectives of Congress."[7]

- **Second, states cannot pass laws inconsistent with the FAA's broad mandate to enforce agreements to arbitrate.**

---

[7]   *Volt Info. Scis., Inc. v. Bd. Of Trustees of Leland Stanford Jr. Univ.*, 489 U.S. 468, 477 (1989) (citations omitted).

The FAA creates an equal-treatment principle:

A court may invalidate an arbitration agreement based on "generally applicable contract defenses" like fraud or unconscionability, but not on legal rules that "apply only to arbitration or that derive their meaning from the fact that an agreement to arbitrate is at issue."[8]

Put more concisely, **the FAA preempts a state law ground** for invalidating an arbitration agreement to the extent the ground:

a)   **Does not apply to contracts generally; or**

b)   **Interferes with fundamental attributes of arbitration.**

States, in other words, cannot discriminate against arbitration agreements and:

- Prohibit outright the arbitration of certain categories of disputes;[9]

- Impose unique formality requirements on arbitration agreements, such as requirements that arbitration clauses include special warning language or appear in a conspicuous font;[10]

---

[8]   *AT&T Mobility LLC v. Concepcion*, 563 U.S. 333, 339 (2011).

[9]   *See, e.g., Southland v. Keating*, 465 U.S. 1 (1984) (preempting a California statute prohibiting the arbitration of certain claims against franchisors by franchisees); *Marmet Health Care Ctr., Inc. v. Brown*, 565 U.S. 530 (2012) (*per curiam*) (preempting a West Virginia Supreme Court holding that the state's public policy prevented predispute arbitration agreements that apply to claims of personal injury or wrongful death against nursing homes).

[10]   *See, e.g., Doctor's Assoc. Inc. v. Casarotto*, 517 U.S. 681 (1996) (preempting a Montana statute and holding that requiring warning language in special large format treated arbitration contracts differently than other contracts, thereby violating the purpose of the FAA).

- Limit the right of parties to exclude class actions in arbitration;[11]

- Disfavor contracts that have the defining features of arbitration agreements;[12] or

- Covertly regulate arbitration under the guise of adjusting general contract law.[13]

- **Third, although the FAA creates a federal substantive right to have disputes resolved by arbitration, it does not create federal question subject matter jurisdiction.**

  There's no doubt that the FAA creates a federal substantive right to have disputes resolved in arbitration. But that substantive right, strangely, does not create federal question jurisdiction for federal courts. In other words, even when the FAA is implicated—which occurs in almost every transaction involving an arbitration clause, given the expansive reading of "involving commerce" in FAA § 1—federal courts only have subject matter jurisdiction over arbitration disputes if they have some other basis for that jurisdiction.

  The Supreme Court has described this state of affairs as "something of an anomaly in the field of federal-court jurisdiction."[14]

---

[11] *AT&T Mobility LLC v. Concepcion*, 563 U.S. 333 (2011).

[12] *Epic Sys. Corp. v. Lewis*, 138 S. Ct. 1612, 1622 (2018) ("[T]his means the saving clause does not save defenses that target arbitration . . . by 'interfer[ing] with fundamental attributes of arbitration.' ") (citations omitted).

[13] *See, e.g., Kindred Nursing Centers, LP v. Clark*, 137 S. Ct. 1421 (2017) (preempting a Kentucky Supreme Court rule allowing an agent to waive a principal's constitutional right to access to public courts and to a trial by jury only if express authority to do so was granted by the principal).

[14] *Moses H. Cone Mem'l Hosp. v. Mercury Constr. Corp.*, 460 U.S. 1, 25 n.32 (1983).

- **Finally, there's some room to debate what parts of the FAA are preemptive.**

FAA § 2 constitutes preemptive federal law. In contrast, FAA §§ 3 and 4 are not directly preemptive, as they are expressly directed at federal courts. Still, as we've seen, functionally equivalent remedies to those provided by FAA §§ 3 and 4 must be available in state courts to vindicate the federal right provided by FAA § 2. So, the spirit of FAA §§ 3 and 4 is preemptive.

It's less clear whether the spirit of FAA §§ 9, 10, and 11 is preemptive. These sections, recall, govern confirmation, review, and enforcement of arbitral awards. The critical question, in terms of preemption, centers on whether the spirit of FAA § 10, which sets the floor and the ceiling of judicial review of arbitral awards, applies in state courts. Dicta suggests that FAA § 10 may not have this sort of preemptive force.

In *Hall Street Associates, L.L.C. v. Mattel, Inc.*, the Supreme Court held that the four FAA § 10 grounds are the exclusive grounds for vacating an arbitral award in federal court. But the Court went on, in dicta, to say that

> [t]he FAA is not the only way into court for parties wanting review of arbitration awards: they may contemplate enforcement under state statutory or common law, for example, where judicial review of different scope is arguable.

In most cases, the available grounds for review and enforcement of arbitral awards under state law are the same as those provided for in FAA § 10, so no preemption issue exists. But some state laws diverge from FAA § 10 and permit either narrower or broader post-award review.

Currently, courts and commentators are split on whether the FAA preempts state law grounds for post-award review and enforcement. The Supreme Court has, to date, declined to address the matter further.

4. State Laws of Arbitration

Every state in the U.S. has enacted some general arbitration law, and several states have adopted specialized arbitration rules applying to international arbitration. Most states have adopted either the Uniform Arbitration Act ("UAA"), which was created in 1955, or the RUAA, which was created in 2000, as their general arbitration law. As of 2018, 23 states have adopted the RUAA, with most of the rest still relying on the UAA.

Given the preemptive force of the FAA, these laws have a somewhat limited role to play in arbitration. Essentially, state laws can perform five functions:

- **Supply generally applicable contract rules used to determine if an arbitration agreement is valid and enforceable.**

  FAA § 2 establishes a vital role for state contract law: it hinges the determination of whether a valid and enforceable arbitration agreement exists on application of generally applicable contract rules.

Accordingly, at least generally applicable state contract law has a key role to play in arbitration.

Look at Revised Uniform Arbitration Act ("RUAA") § 6(a), which incorporates FAA § 2 almost verbatim. Because FAA § 2 is preemptive, the only option for states is to adopt rules that are identical. That's what the RUAA does.

- **Supply the governing arbitration law in purely intrastate transactions.**

  Theoretically, there could be purely intrastate transactions involving arbitration. FAA § 1 would not extend the Act's coverage to such transactions.

  In practice, however, it's almost impossible to conceive of a purely intrastate transaction, given the Supreme Court's generous reading of FAA § 1— "involving commerce"—which extends coverage to the widest scope Congress' power to regulate under the Commerce Clause.

- **Provide applicable procedural arbitration law to the extent that it does not conflict with the FAA.**

  The FAA, as you've seen, is a spare statute that says very little. State law can provide more detailed rules, so long as those additional rules do not conflict with the FAA or the fundamental attributes of arbitration.

  In particular, because FAA §§ 3 and 4 are not applicable in state courts, state law needs to supply remedies for the breach of an arbitration contract when enforcement is sought in state court. State arbitration law must provide functionally equivalent remedies to those available in federal courts.

See, for instance,

- *RUAA § 7—requiring courts to stay pending litigation and compel arbitration if a valid and enforceable arbitration agreement exists.*

Additionally, FAA §§ 5 and 7—which provide for mechanisms that allow federal courts to support and aid the arbitral process—apply only in federal courts. State law could provide similar mechanisms, and perhaps even additional mechanisms.

See, for instance,

- *RUAA § 8—allowing courts to grant provisional remedies, like injunctions, if arbitrators are not yet appointed;*

- *RUAA § 12—articulating standards for disclosure by arbitrators, a subject not addressed in the text of the FAA;*

- *RUAA § 14—providing immunity for arbitrators and arbitral institutions, a subject not addressed in the text of the FAA;*

- *RUAA § 17—allowing arbitrators to borrow certain evidence gathering powers of courts, like FAA § 7 but providing far more detail; and*

- *RUAA § 20—allowing arbitrators to change or correct awards under limited circumstances, a subject not addressed in the text of the FAA.*

- **Provide mechanisms for the review and enforcement of arbitral awards in state courts.**

    FAA §§ 9, 10, and 11 seem to be directed at federal courts and thus may not be preemptive. Accordingly, if parties seek to enforce an arbitral award in state court, state law may need to supply the mechanism for reviewing and enforcing the award.

    As briefly discussed in the previous section on preemption, courts and commentators are divided on whether state law may diverge, substantively, from federal law during the review and enforcement stage. U.S. Supreme Court dicta, some commentators, and several state court decisions, seem to support the notion that states are free to create narrower or broader grounds for review and enforcement. Other court decisions and commentators suggest that states do not have unfettered ability to fashion their own post-award review standards.

    Whatever the theoretical possibilities, the reality is that most courts adopt functionally equivalent rules for the review and enforcement of arbitration awards.

    See for instance:

    - *RUAA § 22—providing rules for confirmation of arbitral awards that works like FAA § 9;*

    - *RUAA § 23—providing rules for review and vacation of arbitral awards that map onto the rules in FAA § 10; and*

- ▪ *RUAA § 24—providing very limited rules for modification and correction of arbitral awards by courts, functionally equivalent to FAA § 11.*

- **Supply other default rules.**

  Parties do not agree on every possible issue in their arbitration agreements. As we have seen, arbitration laws, then, may supply default rules that will fill in gaps in the parties' agreement. The RUAA's drafters recognized this and believed that state law should primarily address default legal rules governing "arbitration procedure," which are virtually non-existent within the FAA.

  See, for instance:

  - ▪ *RUAA § 4—explaining that all rules in the RUAA are defaults unless § 4 specifically provides otherwise and establishing that most of the RUAA constitutes default rules;*

  - ▪ *RUAA § 15—describing the default rules governing how an arbitral process should function, a subject not addressed in the text of the FAA; and*

  - ▪ *RUAA § 21—discussing the remedial power of arbitrators and the default rules regarding.*

CHAPTER 5

Arbitration Institutions and Rules

Parties can create bespoke agreements and processes each time they decide to arbitrate. That's called *ad hoc* arbitration. There can be significant advantages to the freedom and customization possible with *ad hoc* arbitration.

But *ad hoc* arbitration can also be a lot of work. Parties are responsible for managing not only the details of their individual arguments and cases but also the dispute resolution process generally.

When parties don't want to do everything themselves, they turn to arbitration institutions for help.

There are many arbitration institutions around the world. Some of the leading institutions in the United States include the non-profit American Arbitration Association ("AAA") and the International Institute for Conflict Prevention & Resolution ("CPR"), and the for-profit JAMS (which originally stood for "Judicial Arbitration and Mediation Services"). Some global institutions include the International Chamber of Commerce ("ICC"), the London Court of International Arbitration ("LCIA"), the Singapore

International Arbitration Centre ("SIAC"), and the AAA's International Centre for Dispute Resolution ("ICDR"). And these are only a handful of institutions that exist both domestically and internationally.

Each of these institutions typically offers their own set of rules and their own menu of additional services. While there's a lot of variety among the offerings, institutions can provide parties with at least three benefits:

- **Procedural rules**—rather than writing the rules governing the process of arbitration, parties can incorporate by reference a set of pre-fabricated institutional rules into their agreement.

- **Arbitrator lists**—rather than having to find and vet arbitrators themselves, parties may turn to an institution for help. Most institutions have lists of arbitrators who have been vetted by the institution.

- **Administrative services**—rather than managing all the administrative complications of an arbitration themselves, parties can hire institutions to administer the arbitration.

Of course, arbitration institutions charge for most of these benefits. (Most institutions have their rules publicly available, so it is possible for parties to "borrow" the rules without paying for them.) The fees charged by arbitration institutions for their services must be tacked onto the fees charged by the arbitrators.

1. Procedural Rules

Institutions publish sets of rules that parties may adopt as part of their arbitration agreement. Importantly, these rules are merely incorporated by reference into the agreement. They have no independent force or authority. These rules, in other words, merely become part of the parties' agreement, if and when the parties agree to use them.

So, why would parties ever agree to use these rules? There are a number of good reasons, but not least among them is that the rules represent a thoughtfully-developed set of procedures, which have been tested in numerous arbitral proceedings. Rather than expend the time, money and effort to craft their own bespoke rules, parties often find it easier to pick a tried-and-true set of rules. This reduces transaction costs and minimizes the possibility of collateral disputes about the procedures themselves.

While every institution advertises that their rules offer particular benefits, and every rule set may have some unique features, arbitration rules tend to focus on similar subjects:

- procedures for initiating the arbitration;

- methods and processes for picking arbitrators;

- the timing and role of any pre-hearing conferences;

- information exchanges and evidence gathering;

- any motion practices;

- powers of the arbitrator;

- the conduct and structure of the hearing;

- arbitral awards and remedies; and

- procedures for publication or clarification of awards.

Again, this is a generic list. Particular arbitration rules may include other subjects, including things like optional appellate-like review processes, confidentiality, and emergency arbitrator services for things like preliminary relief before an arbitral tribunal is constituted.

The critical point to remember is that these rules are nothing more or less than the agreement of the parties about how the arbitration will be conducted. That can feel a bit awkward, especially to lawyers unaccustomed to thinking of procedural rules this way. Most institutional rules read like civil rules of procedure in public courts, so they can seem more official than they actually are.

It's possible for parties to alter the rules, at least to some degree. If parties alter the rules too much, an arbitration institution may refuse to administer the arbitration, but otherwise, parties have the same freedom of contract with the rules as they do with any other aspect of their arbitration agreement.

2. Arbitrator Lists

Practically, parties get a lot of bang for their buck from institutions' arbitrator lists. Most institutions vet prospective arbitrators and then sponsor lists of "qualified" people to serve on particular cases.

Parties can save time, money, and effort by paying for the intermediary services of an institution which has already evaluated the general suitability of arbitrators. Parties, then, focus their efforts on selecting from a qualified group of prospective arbitrators the best person for their particular needs.

Institutional arbitrator lists vary considerably—more, perhaps, than institutional rules vary. For example, some institutions include only arbitrators with legal or judicial backgrounds on their panels, while others sponsor panels with a much greater diversity of experiences. Some institutions have a velvet-rope approach to the application and screening processes for prospective arbitrators, practically assuring that any arbitrators they recommend have impeccable credentials, experience, or both. Other institutions are more permissive with who they will accept as prospective arbitrators, but they offer parties a greater range of arbitrator fees to choose from.

In addition to the actual lists of prospective arbitrators, some institutions also provide detailed ethical rules governing the service of arbitrators. These rules supplement the general requirements of arbitration law and function as a form of self-regulation. Arbitrators who fail to abide by these stricter or more specific requirements may be removed from an institution's list of available arbitrators.

Finally, many institutions will help parties with the selection process itself, winnowing the possibilities for a prospective arbitrator or even selecting an arbitrator for the parties.

3. Administrative Services

Arbitration institutions can provide considerable administrative support to the parties and the arbitrators. Like rules and arbitrator lists, the administrative services institutions offer can vary greatly, but as a general matter, many institutions help with:

- The transmission of communications between parties and arbitrators;

- Managing the scheduling needs of parties and arbitrators;

- Organizing the physical space or technologies required for pre-hearing conferences and hearings;

- Handling the details of collecting arbitrator fees from parties and getting arbitrators paid;

- Putting arbitral awards into a final and consistent form and making sure that they are appropriately edited; and

- Sometimes even engaging in some minimal review of awards to make sure that the award is likely to be enforceable.

Without an institution involved, parties must deal with these work-a-day issues themselves. Of course, these services are not free. *Ad hoc* arbitration avoids or minimizes fees and offers potential flexibility in the structuring and management of the arbitration process.

Self-administered or *ad hoc* arbitrations can work well in circumstances where the parties find themselves regularly squabbling over relatively minor issues. In these situations, parties can create their own norms and processes for expediting resolution of their disputes. Self-administered arbitrations might also be beneficial in cases where the parties are very serious about confidentiality, wanting to limit the number of eyes that have even the slightest access to their dispute. It's also possible to imagine self-administered arbitrations in situations where the parties are willing and able to agree on the selection of an extremely experienced arbitrator or chair who can self-manage administrative details.

CHAPTER 6

Enforcing Arbitration Agreements

If a valid arbitration contract exists, arbitration law holds parties to their promises to forgo courts and instead adjudicate their disputes before an arbitrator. Arbitration law then enforces the arbitrator's award.

Those two functions—enforcement of arbitration agreements and enforcement of arbitral awards—are the subjects of this Chapter and the next. As discussed in Chapter 4, these functions are the primary and mandatory rules provided by arbitration law.

This Chapter will focus on the first function of arbitration law: enforcing the agreement to arbitration.

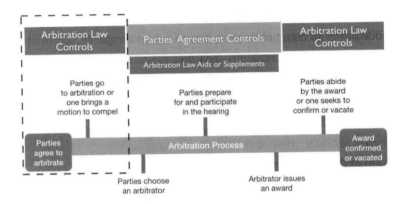

With respect to enforcement of the agreement, arbitration law can be seen as a subspecies of contract law. In fact, as you saw in Chapter 4, FAA § 2 specifically incorporates general state contract law, making arbitration agreements enforceable to the same extent as any other contracts. FAA § 2 makes it impossible for states to discriminate against arbitration contracts, but it also makes arbitration contracts subject to the same generally-applicable rules as other contracts.

In brief, arbitration contracts will be enforceable if:

1. The subject matter of the dispute is arbitrable (subject matter arbitrability exists); and

2. A valid, written arbitration contract meeting the minimum requirements of generally-applicable state contract law exists and covers the dispute (contractual arbitrability exists).

   a. Is the arbitration agreement valid and enforceable (or are there flaws in the agreement)?

   b. Does the dispute fall within the scope of the arbitration agreement?

c.   Are all procedural preconditions to arbitration satisfied?

If the subject matter of a dispute is arbitrable and an enforceable arbitration contract exists covering that dispute, arbitration law dictates that a court must stay any pending litigation and send the parties to arbitration.

Things can get more complicated, however, for a couple of reasons. First, as Chapter 3 discussed, arbitration law adds a twist. Specifically, arbitration law includes the concept of separability. Second, as Chapter 3 also discussed, the concept of kompentenz-kompentenz jumbles up which decision-maker, a court or the arbitrator, decides certain questions of contractual arbitrability.

This Chapter breaks down the process of enforcing an arbitration agreement in greater detail, aiming to help you see how these various pieces fit together.   Because subject matter arbitrability is hardly ever a concern in the U.S., this Chapter does not address it beyond this introduction.

1.   To Go to Arbitration or Not to Go to Arbitration, That's the Question

An arbitration may address two or sometimes three related conflicts.   There's always a conflict about the merits of a dispute (Conflict 1).   That's the dispute that the parties are really focused on and care about.   But arbitration may also need to address a conflict over arbitrability—a conflict about whether an arbitrator has authority to resolve the merits dispute (Conflict 2).   If that wasn't enough, arbitration may also involve a conflict over which decision maker—a court or an arbitrator—gets to decide the conflict over arbitrability (Conflict 3).

These three interlocking conflicts need to be resolved in reverse order.   Before we can get to resolving the merits of a dispute, we need to figure out if an arbitrator has the authority to resolve the merits. And before we can decide if the arbitrator has authority to resolve the merits, we need to decide who is going to make that decision.

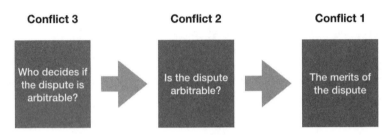

Importantly, parties may simply agree, at the outset of a dispute, to go to arbitration. If they do, they are skipping at least Conflict 3. They might also agree that the dispute is arbitrable, thereby skipping Conflict 2. In those easy cases, the arbitrator can simply get to work on the heart of the case and resolve the dispute over the merits.

But things aren't always easy, especially when parties are in a fighting mood.

If one party refuses to participate in arbitration, the other may need to turn to a court for help. If that happens, a court considering a motion to compel (and stay any pending litigation) will have to begin with Conflict 3.

A. Who Decides if the Dispute Is Arbitrable? (Conflict 3)

Arbitration law has two doctrines that focus on helping resolve the "who decides?" conflict. You've already seen both: separability and kompentenz-kompentenz. These doctrines function to make sure that parties who have chosen to arbitrate have their disputes funneled into arbitration as quickly and seamlessly as possible. But these doctrines also recognize that a party resisting arbitration may be doing so precisely because she did not agree to arbitrate. So, these doctrines have to balance arbitral efficiency against the risk that a party might be forced to arbitrate against her will.

i.   Separability

Separability technically doesn't address the "who decides?" conflict, but practically it helps restrict the options a party has to resist arbitration. In other words, separability narrows the possible set of complaints that a party can make to a court about the arbitration contract. Separability pushes most contract-related issues to the arbitrator.

Separability applies to the first branch of contractual arbitrability: flaws in the arbitration contract. In other words, separability applies when a party resists arbitration by complaining that the arbitration agreement has a flaw that renders it invalid or unenforceable.

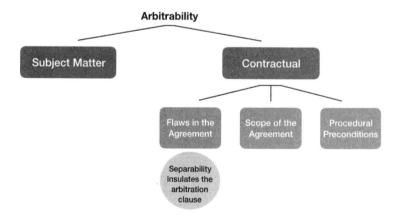

Recall from Chapter 3 that separability means that arbitral clauses must be treated as analytically distinct from the container contracts in which they usually appear. Promises to arbitrate are independent and separate from whatever other substantive commitments parties have made.

Unless a party specifically challenges the validity of arbitration clause itself—as opposed to the container contract—the dispute remains arbitrable. Allegations of contractual invalidity made against the main contract do not necessarily taint the arbitral clause. The challenging party must establish that the alleged invalidity bears directly upon the arbitral clause.

ii.   Kompentenz-Kompentenz

The international concept of kompentenz-kompentenz addresses the "who decides?" issue directly. As you might recall from Chapter 3, however, U.S. law has a kompentenz-kompentenz concept only in a slightly roundabout way.

a)   Flaws in the Agreement and Scope of the Agreement

In U.S. law, if a party alleges a flaw in the arbitration agreement specifically, a court presumptively has the authority and obligation to decide if the dispute is arbitrable. Similarly, if a party resists arbitration on the ground that the particular dispute does not fall within the scope of the arbitral clause, a court presumptively has the authority and obligation to decide if the dispute is arbitrable.

But parties may delegate authority to arbitrators to decide both forms of contractual arbitrability in "clear and unmistakable" language. These delegations effectively give arbitrators the power to rule on their own jurisdiction and thus allow parties to opt into the concept of kompentenz-kompentenz.

If a delegation clause exists, the parties have chosen to have an arbitrator decide Conflict 2. In the face of a delegation clause, a court, considering Conflict 3, has essentially three tasks:

- **Determine if the delegation is "clear and unmistakable" language.** Courts have gotten pretty permissive about what they will accept as sufficiently "clear and unmistakable" language for a delegation clause. Courts almost universally agree that the delegation clause may be found in institutional rules incorporated by reference into the arbitration clause. Many institutions, including the AAA and JAMS, have rules that sufficiently delegate authority to arbitrators to decide jurisdictional issues.

- **Determine if the claim of arbitrability is wholly groundless.** Some courts refuse to honor delegation clauses if the party wanting to proceed to arbitration has a wholly groundless basis for asserting that contractual arbitrability exists. The wholly groundless doctrine gives courts the opportunity to conduct a sort of gateway smell test. If the party who wants to arbitrate has a completely outlandish basis for doing so, some courts will look past the formalism of a delegation clause.

  Importantly, the wholly groundless doctrine is currently the subject of a Circuit split, and the U.S. Supreme Court has taken a case for its 2019 term to resolve the confusion.[1]

- **Determine if the delegation clause itself has a contract flaw.** In what has been described as a Russian nesting-doll problem, a party could, in theory, challenge the validity of the delegation

---

[1] *Henry Schein Inc. v. Archer and White Sales Inc.*, 138 S. Ct. 2678 (2018) (granting certiorari).

clause itself. The U.S. Supreme Court has said, however, that delegation clauses are separable from the arbitration clauses that contain them.[2] In other words, the separability doctrine makes arbitration clauses analytically independent of container contracts, but it also makes delegation clauses analytically independent from both the overarching container contract and from the rest of the arbitration clause. As a result, identifying a flaw that targets the delegation clause specifically can be almost impossible.

b)   Procedural Preconditions

No delegation clause is needed to know that arbitrators get to decide one category of contractual arbitrability questions: questions about whether a procedural precondition has been satisfied. If a party challenging an arbitration agreement has done so on the basis that a precondition was not satisfied, the challenge must be heard and decided by the arbitrator.

iii.   Putting the Pieces Together

Simplified, a court will decide Conflict 2—whether the dispute is arbitrable—if:

- The party resisting arbitration attacks the arbitration clause specifically on the grounds that either a flaw makes it invalid or unenforceable or the particular dispute is not covered by the arbitral clause; and

- No delegation clause exists, or the delegation clause is unenforceable.

---

[2]   *Rent-A-Ctr., W., Inc. v. Jackson,* 561 U.S. 63 (2010).

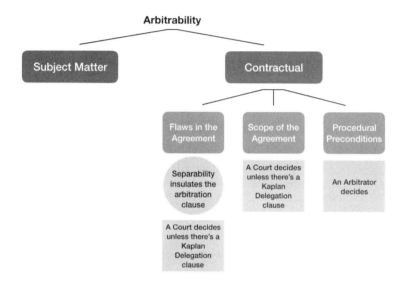

B. Is the Dispute Arbitrable? (Conflict 2)

As Chapter 3 discussed, contractual arbitrability breaks down into three sub-questions:

- **Are there flaws in the agreement?** Does a valid and enforceable contract to arbitrate exist?

- **Does the dispute fall within the scope of the agreement?** Assuming that a valid arbitration contract exists, did the parties commit to arbitrate the specific dispute at issue?

- **Are there any preconditions to the right to arbitrate?** Assuming that a valid arbitration contract exists, are there any conditions to the right to arbitrate that have not been satisfied?

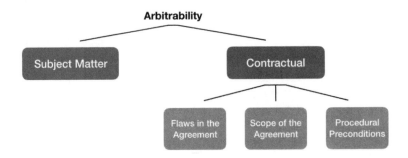

Let's consider these three branches in a bit more detail.

i.   Flaws in the Agreement

Arbitration agreements are treated as regular contracts. Accordingly, arbitration agreements must meet the formation requirements for contracts and must not be subject to any generally applicable contract defenses.

In the spirit of this Guide, we'll keep this review of contract law brief.

a)   Formation Requirements

Formation of a contract requires: (1) mutual assent; and (2) consideration.

Mutual assent usually amounts to an offer and an acceptance. But in the real word of transactions, those two components often blur. The point is that parties must be voluntarily agreeing to arbitrate. That agreement can be manifested in a variety of ways, but contract law focuses on the "objective" manifestations of the parties, not their subjective intentions. In other words, we do not really care what parties intend in their own heads. Instead, we care about what a reasonable person outside of their heads would understand from their words and actions.

With respect to arbitration agreements in particular, a few common mutual assent issues can arise in the following contexts:

- **Mass Market Boilerplate**—Most contracts in the modern world arise from mass market transactions where a commercial party drafts boilerplate terms and sells goods or services, or offers employment, pursuant to those terms on a take-it-or-leave-it basis. Individuals have little or no room to negotiate or bargain about the terms. Perhaps as a result, few individuals even read the boilerplate.

  As Chapter 8 discusses in greater detail, mutual assent in such a situation can only be hypothetical. Individuals cannot actually be agreeing to the terms, if they've never seen them or if they do not understand them.

  Nevertheless, most courts, most of the time, conclude that so long as individuals had reasonable notice of the terms and an opportunity to review them if they wanted to do so, they will be held to those terms if they go ahead with the transaction.

- **Assent Through Agents**—Agents can bind their principals to contracts under certain circumstances. But those circumstances can be tricky. Issues can arise when one party agrees to a contract on behalf of someone else. As a very general matter, an agent can bind a principal when she has actual or apparent authority to do so, but the details of such authority can be fact intensive.

- **Assent Through Exchanges of Forms**—Many law students cringe at the recollection of the so-called battle of the forms and Section 2–207 of the Uniform Commercial Code. Relax. That's well beyond the scope of this Guide. But the idea, in brief, is that assent may be found through the parties' exchanges of forms, even if those forms do not mirror one another, at least in some circumstances. Courts faced with arbitration agreements allegedly formed through a "battle of the forms" have divided on whether mutual assent exists.

Of course, other issues related to mutual assent may also arise.

In contrast to mutual assent, consideration issues rarely arise. Consideration exists, quite simply, when each side to a transaction is getting something from the other in the deal. Commonly, in arbitration agreements, each side is getting the other's promise to arbitrate. Most arbitration agreements are reciprocal. Those pose absolutely no consideration concerns.

Sometimes, however, an arbitration agreement will be one-sided. In those cases, there must be some other consideration to support the promise to arbitrate.

b) Defenses Enforcement or Excuses for Non-Performance

There are a number of general defenses to contracts or excuses for non-performance, including fraud, duress, undue influence, unconscionability, illegality, frustration of purpose, impracticability, and mistake. Most of these defenses or excuses, however, are filtered out by the separability doctrine, most of the time.

Unless one of these defenses is aimed directly at the arbitration provision, the separability doctrine protects the arbitrability of the dispute. In other words, an arbitrator will decide if the defense undermines the container contract as part of a decision on the merits of the dispute.

The defense most likely to invalidate the arbitration agreement itself is unconscionability. Unconscionability applies in a somewhat amorphous range of situations, often where other process defects like fraud or duress cannot quite be proven. Under the doctrine, courts will refuse to enforce a contract if, on balance, the combination of the bargaining process and the terms in the contract are so one-sided as to "shock the conscience." The unconscionability doctrine, in other words, is divided into procedural unconscionability and substantive unconscionability. Procedural unconscionability focuses on the bargaining process. Substantive unconscionability focuses on a particular provision within the contract.

Importantly, unconscionability arguments only fly if there's a significant disparity in bargaining power. While adhesive agreements are not *per se* unconscionable, basically only adhesive contracts might be unconscionable. Accordingly, unconscionability is discussed in more detail in Chapter 8.

ii. Scope of the Agreement

Even if a valid contract for arbitration exists, parties might decide to exempt specific disputes or categories of disputes from arbitration. In other words, parties might carve out certain matters and reserve them for resolution in public courts.

Determining the scope of an arbitration agreement requires interpreting it. The primary objective in interpreting any contract is to ascertain the intentions of the parties. With regard to arbitration agreements specifically, many courts begin the interpretive process by classifying the clause as "broad" or "narrow."

Broad clauses often use the words "any and all disputes" or "any disputes arising out of or related to the contract." These sorts of words are not magical incantations, but they are routinely interpreted by courts as indicating that the parties want to arbitrate as much as they possibly can. Accordingly, if a court concludes that an arbitral clause is "broad," courts employ a presumption that even claims collateral to or remote from the container contract are arbitrable.

Narrow clauses, in contrast, evidence that the parties wanted to exclude one or more matters from arbitrability. If the parties use any sort of carveout language, a court may conclude that the clause is "narrow" in scope. Narrow clauses do not benefit from the presumption given to broad clauses. Instead, courts are much more attentive to the precise language used by the parties, and they scrutinize the entire contract to try and distinguish between what, specifically, the parties wanted to arbitrate and what, specifically, they wanted to exclude from the reach of arbitration.

iii. Procedural Preconditions

The parties may impose preconditions on their obligation to arbitrate or the circumstances may be such that a precondition should be implied into the contract. As discussed back in Chapter 3, a precondition amounts to some sort of event that must occur before the time to perform the promise to arbitrate comes due.

Importantly, arbitrators always have the power and responsibility to decide if a precondition exists and if it has been satisfied.

2. An Example

Imagine two parties to an arbitration agreement.

Dom is a private detective. He has entered into a contract with Northwest Security Solutions, Inc. (NSS), agreeing to provide certain investigation and security support services as an independent contractor. The contract contains a broad arbitration clause, purporting to obligate Dom to arbitrate "any and all" claims that he might have against NSS. The agreement also contains a provision saying that the arbitrator has jurisdiction to decide "all jurisdictional disputes." The agreement says nothing about NSS having to arbitrate claims it might have against Dom.

A dispute arises between Dom and NSS regarding services Dom has provided. Dom claims that he did the work appropriately and in conformity with his obligations under the contract. NSS, on the other hand, says that the work was shoddy and did not live up to the quality promised by Dom. It's refusing to pay him. Dom threatens to bring a claim to get paid.

Of course, Dom and NSS might try to settle their dispute through any of the facilitative dispute resolution mechanisms available—negotiation or mediation, for instance. Let's assume that such efforts at resolution fail. The parties need to adjudicate their differences.

But let's imagine that Dom does not want to arbitrate. Accordingly, he files a lawsuit in a public court. NSS responds to the lawsuit with a motion to stay the lawsuit and compel arbitration.

In opposing the motion, Dom argues that the arbitration agreement is flawed because it is unconscionable and it was not supported by consideration. It's unconscionable, he says, because it imposed a one-sided obligation to arbitrate on only him. It did not bind NSS to go to arbitration. The one-sidedness is substantively problematic. Moreover, the one-sidedness indicates that there was no consideration given by NSS to support Dom's promise to arbitrate.

NSS, of course, disagrees with Dom's arguments. But for our purposes, the real question is who will decide if Dom's complaints render the dispute inarbitrable? Note that we are starting at Conflict 3—who decides if the dispute is arbitrable—the court or the arbitrator?

Dom challenges the contractual arbitrability of the dispute. Specifically, he's arguing that there are two flaws in the arbitration contract. So, the first thing that we should think about is whether the doctrine of separability will apply and push these issues to the arbitrator. Here it will not apply.

With respect to Dom's unconscionability argument, he has focused on the arbitration clause specifically. He's saying that the fact that the clause is one-sided makes it substantively unconscionable. Because he's not attacking the validity of the container contract generally but instead is targeting the arbitration clause specifically, separability does not apply.

Similarly, with respect to his lack of consideration argument, he has focused on the arbitration clause specifically. He's saying that his promise to arbitrate didn't get him anything from NSS in return. As a result, he's arguing, the arbitration promise is not legally enforceable. Separability does not apply.

The next question we need to ask, then, is whether a delegation provision exists. It does. The delegation provision says that the arbitrator has jurisdiction to decide "all jurisdictional disputes." If this clause is effective, it means that the parties wanted an arbitrator to decide all questions of contractual arbitrability.

The clause will be effective if it: (1) uses clear and unmistakable language; (2) does not relate to a wholly groundless claim of arbitrability by NSS; and (3) is not, itself, contractually flawed.

Probably Dom's best argument would be to focus on (1) and try to argue that the language is not sufficiently clear and unmistakable. This, however, will likely be a losing battle. Though the clause does not use the term "arbitrability" it does use the term "jurisdiction." Most courts would likely find the terms sufficiently synonymous to demonstrate the parties' intentions to send questions of arbitrability to the arbitrator.

NSS's claim of arbitrability does not appear to be outlandish or "wholly groundless." The arbitration contract specifically says that any and all claims by Dom must be arbitrated. It's far from clear that Dom can or should prevail and, in any event, NSS is not overreaching in wanting to arbitrate this particular dispute.

Finally, Dom probably hasn't done enough to challenge the validity of the delegation clause as opposed the arbitration clause. This is a tricky one, and it's not entirely clear what more Dom could do or would need to do. But Dom's unconscionability argument focuses on the arbitration provision as a whole. He does not seem to be alleging that there is anything specifically unconscionable about delegating the authority to determine arbitrability to the arbitrator. Remember, delegation clauses are separable from the arbitration clause just like the arbitration clause is separable from the container contract. In this case, it does not look like Dom has targeted the delegation clause specifically. Similarly, Dom's lack of consideration argument focuses on the arbitration clause as a whole, not on the delegation clause specifically.

Because the delegation clause looks to be valid, the court should grant NSS's motion, stay the pending litigation and compel Dom to go to arbitration.

Importantly, Dom can still make both his objections to contractual arbitrability before the arbitrator. But the court should not decide those matters on the front end of the arbitral process.

We don't have enough information to be sure how Conflict 2 will be resolved by the arbitrator, but it's worth noting that both arguments are a toss-up. If Dom can persuade the arbitrator that the bargaining power between him and NSS was not equal, it's possible that he could prevail on the unconscionability argument.

As Chapter 8 will discuss, courts are generally skeptical of one-sided arbitration clauses. Dom's lack-of-consideration argument is a tougher sell, but he might be able to persuade the arbitrator that he got nothing in return for his promise to arbitrate.

CHAPTER 7

Enforcing Arbitral Awards

The Chapter 6 addressed the front-end role of mandatory arbitration law: enforcing agreements to arbitrate. This Chapter turns to a closer evaluation of the back-end role of mandatory arbitration law: enforcing arbitral awards.

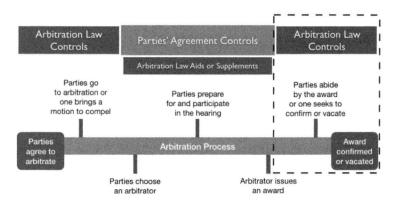

Parties may voluntarily comply with an arbitral award. After all, arbitration only occurs when the parties have chosen it, and if they have, that usually means that they want to avoid courts. If parties comply with the award, no further judicial action is needed.

Of course, things aren't always so easy. One party—usually the loser—might not be satisfied with the award. Such a disgruntled party could seek to vacate the award in court, or she could simply toss it in the trash. Remember, arbitrators have no state-sanctioned judicial powers. Their awards are really just pieces of paper.

If the losing party disregards an arbitral award, the winning party may go to court and have the award confirmed, thereby converting it into a court judgment. With a judgment in hand, the winning party can use the coercive police power of the state for enforcement. This means the winner may obtain judicial liens on property and garnishments, among other things.

Vacatur and confirmation are two sides of the same coin. It's usual for both motions to be made simultaneously. One party seeks to confirm and the other seeks to vacate or vice versa. Both motions involve a court reviewing the arbitral award and determining whether it is judicially enforceable.

This Chapter explores the details of judicial enforcement of arbitral awards. The upshot is that courts are quite deferential to arbitrators and to the arbitral process. It's a rare occasion when a court vacates an award.

1. The Preclusive Effect of Enforceable Arbitral Awards

If something's been arbitrated, it generally cannot be relitigated. In other words, arbitral awards may have preclusive effect, unless and until they are vacated.

Preclusion can be its own bewildering area of law. The law of preclusion deals with the effect of a lawsuit on future litigation. We don't need to untangle all of knots. For our purposes, it's enough to say that there are two branches of preclusion: Claim preclusion (often referred to as res judicata) and issue preclusion (often referred to as collateral estoppel).[1]

A. *Claim Preclusion*

Arbitral awards have claim-preclusive effect. Claim preclusion bars a party from bringing a second claim seeking relief for the same dispute against the same counter-party. The claim-preclusive effect of an arbitral award attaches whether or not a court has confirmed the award.

Imagine that Millie and Tueller have entered into an arbitration agreement. Millie brings a claim against Tueller in arbitration for negligence and the arbitrator rules in Millie's favor. Unhappy with the result, Tueller then initiates a second arbitration against Millie addressing the same matter. The arbitrator should rule for Millie without a second thought. The claim has already been decided in the first arbitration.

Claim preclusion for arbitral awards makes good sense. Without it, the final and binding nature of arbitration would be imperiled. Arbitral awards should have the same claim preclusive effect as court judgments. Otherwise, arbitration could be seen as an inferior and less certain mode of adjudication.

B. *Issue Preclusion*

Arbitral awards may have issue-preclusive effect, at the discretion of a judge or arbitrator. Unlike claim preclusion, issue preclusion does not bar an entire claim. Instead, it bars repeated disputes about factual or legal issues within a claim. Issue preclusion prevents a party from rehashing a particular issue that

---

[1] Sometimes the preclusion rules are collectively, and very confusingly, referred to as res judicata. *See, e.g., Taylor v. Sturgell,* 553 U.S. 880, 886, n.5 (2008) (defining claim and issue preclusion as being collectively referred to as "res judicata"). You can never go wrong, however, with calling the two branches claim and issue preclusion.

has already been fully and fairly determined in a previous case. While issue preclusion can only be asserted *against* someone who was a party to the prior case, it can be asserted *by* someone who was a stranger to that prior case.

Consider Tueller and Millie again. Millie brings a claim against Tueller in arbitration for negligence, and the arbitrator rules in her favor. Now imagine that Tyron sues Tueller in public court for an injury arising out of the same conduct that the arbitrator decided amounted to negligence by Tueller. The court may adopt the arbitrator's conclusion that Tueller's conduct failed to comply with a duty of care that he owed. In other words, the court may adopt the arbitrator's conclusions about the facts and law establishing some of the elements of negligence. Tyron may not need to re-establish these facts and legal conclusions.

Issue preclusion exists to prevent socially wasteful fighting over issues already decided by a competent adjudicator after a party has had a fair opportunity to be heard. But issue preclusion, even in public courts, presents a couple of serious risks. First, it incentivizes some potential plaintiffs to sit on the sidelines while others expend resources and time to litigate, creating a free-rider problem. Think about Tyron in the previous example. He can benefit, from Millie's time and effort establishing Tueller's negligence, but he doesn't have to pay anything for this benefit. That means that people in Tyron's position might wait around hoping that they can ride the coattails of people in Millie's position who will do the hard work of proving issues for them.

In addition to this free-rider problem, issue preclusion can create serious due process concerns. Factual and legal issues do not always come up in identical ways in different disputes. What might seem like a fairly minor issue in one dispute could turn out to be of critical importance in another. An effected party who might not have invested sufficient energy fighting about the issue in the first case could wind up being haunted by that choice later.

Issue preclusion in arbitration presents an additional concern. Not all awards are backed by written reasons or findings. In the absence of a written explanation of the award's conclusions, it can be difficult for a subsequent decision maker to determine the propriety of issue preclusion.

Because of these problems, issue preclusion is always a matter of discretion for a subsequent adjudicator.

2. Litigating About Arbitration: Trusting Arbitrators

Courts generally don't second guess arbitrators. That's the critical message of the remainder of this Chapter.

A tightly constrained review of arbitral awards protects the autonomy and efficiency of the arbitral process. As one court colorfully explained, "[a]rbitrators do not act as junior varsity trial courts where subsequent appellate review is readily available to the losing party." Motions to confirm or vacate should not become mere prologues to protracted litigation—which is what arbitration strives to avoid in the first place. Parties who have chosen to resolve their disputes through arbitration need to live with the outcome of that process. Accordingly, courts focus on whether the arbitrators did the job they were told to do—not whether they did it well, or correctly, or reasonably, but simply whether they did it.

In fact, courts are much more deferential to arbitral awards than appellate courts are to the judgments of a lower court. Appellate courts typically review trial courts' factual findings only if they are clearly erroneous and revise procedural choices only if the lower court abused its discretion. But appellate courts review legal determinations by trial courts *de novo*—without any deference. In contrast, courts respect all of the decisions of an arbitrator. The arbitrator's findings of fact, procedural decisions, and conclusions of law are given near total deference. Courts will only vacate an award when there has been an extreme departure from procedural fairness or the arbitrators have egregiously departed from the scope of their authority.

Significantly, unlike many other aspects of modern arbitration law, this extremely deferential approach to arbitral awards is not new. Although courts were hostile to arbitration for many years before and even after passage of the FAA, if an arbitral award was issued, courts would not undermine the arbitrator's decision. This consistent approach to awards has been part of U.S. law for more than 150 years.

At this stage in history, U.S. courts' review of domestic arbitral awards focuses on four issues:

- Corruption, fraud or undue means in the procurement of the arbitral award;

- Evident partiality and bias of the arbitrators;

- Procedural misconduct of the arbitrators in failing to hear material evidence or otherwise prejudicing a party's reasonable opportunity to be heard;

- Situations where the arbitrators exceed their powers.

In addition to these four well-founded grounds for review of arbitral awards, some federal and state courts continue to find that a court may vacate an arbitral award where:

- The arbitrator manifestly disregards the law.

A. Fraud, Corruption, or Undue Means

Things have to go terribly wrong for a court to vacate an award on the basis that it was procured by fraud, corruption, or undue means.

FAA § 10(a)(1) and RUAA 23(a)(1) establish that this sort of radical procedural impropriety may serve as the ground for a court to vacate an arbitral award. To avoid an award, however, courts require essentially four things:

1.   There must be a close causal nexus between the bad behavior—fraud, corruption, or undue means—and the award;

2.   The wrongdoing must not have been discoverable through reasonable diligence before the award;

3.   The wrongdoing must be materially related to an issue in the arbitration; and

4.   The wrongdoing must be established by clear and convincing evidence.

Additionally, in most instances, the arbitrators must not have already considered the allegations of wrongdoing. As these requirements suggest, courts are reluctant to vacate awards for fraud, corruption, or undue means absent dire circumstances.

B. Evident Partiality and Bias of Arbitrators

Arbitrators must be neutral and independent adjudicators. But arbitration law focuses on the evident partiality of arbitrators more than on actual bias. See FAA § 10(a)(2) or RUAA § 23(a)(2)(A)-(B). Courts can investigate whether arbitrators were actually biased, but they rarely do so. The term "evident" centers the discussion on the appearance of partiality. That, in turn, means that the real issue is whether the parties reasonably perceived the arbitrators to be impartial.

Why this focus on perceptions rather than reality?

In significant part it stems from an inherent tension in arbitration. Recall, arbitration requires that a third-party neutral serve as the decision maker. Parties have a right to be judged impartially. But this right can tug against another fundamental attribute of arbitration—the parties' right to choose their arbitrator. There's a tradeoff, in short, between impartiality and expertise. As Judge Richard Posner has noted, an "expert adjudicator is more likely than a judge or juror not only to be precommitted to a particular substantive position but to know or have heard of the parties (or if the parties are organizations, their key people)."[2] The commentary to the RUAA echoes this, adding

> The problem of arbitrator partiality is a difficult one because consensual arbitration involves a tension between abstract concepts of impartial justice and the notion that parties are entitled to a decision maker of their own choosing, including an expert with the biases and prejudices inherent in particular worldly experience.

Arbitration law balances these sometimes-competing attributes of arbitration by requiring that arbitrators disclose to parties all information that might reasonably be seen as affecting their impartiality. The parties can then make an informed choice about whether they have qualms with a particular personal, social, financial, or professional conflict of interest.

---

[2] *Merit Insurance Co. v. Leatherby Insurance Co.*, 714 F.2d 673 (7th Cir. 1983).

Five important points are worth making:

- **Arbitrators have an affirmative duty to investigate and disclose matters that could reasonably be seen as constituting conflicts of interest.**

  An arbitrator has a duty to investigate and disclose facts that a reasonable person would consider likely to affect the arbitrator's impartiality in the arbitral proceeding. What particular dealings or relationships trigger a duty to disclose are highly fact-specific. As a general matter, the two most concerning conflicts involve:

  1. A direct and material interest—certainly a financial interest, though other interests might be relevant as well—in the outcome of the arbitration; or

  2. An existing and substantial relationship with a party.

- **Arbitrators have an on-going duty to investigate and disclose, throughout the arbitral process.**

  Arbitrators aren't off the hook just because they investigated and disclosed at the start of the arbitration. Arbitration law requires that the arbitrators remain vigilant throughout the process.

  For instance, I recently consulted on an arbitration. My name had not appeared on any filings or records, but I showed up to the final hearing to observe. The arbitrator asked who I was, so the lead counsel for our client introduced me. At that point, the arbitrator immediately disclosed to everyone in the hearing that she serves as an adjunct instructor at the law school where I teach. We didn't know one another, but the arbitrator was rightfully attentive to the fact that the overlap in our circles of professional and personal connections could matter to someone.

- **If arbitrators do not disclose a fact, courts may presume that the fact constitutes evident partiality and use that as a basis for vacating the award.**

Arbitration law creates a strong incentive for arbitrators to disclose. If a party later discovers a non-disclosed conflict, a court may presume that the conflict demonstrates evident partiality, even if the conflict seems relatively minor. It then becomes the burden of the party seeking to enforce the award to rebut the presumption by showing that the award was not tainted by the non-disclosure or there in fact was no prejudice.

In essence, this is what happened in the U.S. Supreme Court's decision in *Commonwealth Coatings Corp. v. Continental Casualty Co.*, 393 U.S. 145 (1968). There, an arbitrator's failure to disclose a business relationship with one of the parties was sufficient to support judicial vacation of an arbitration award on the ground of "evident partiality." The case involved an arbitration tribunal made up of two arbitrators chosen by each of the parties and a third "neutral" arbitrator who had previously had a business relationship with one of the parties to the arbitration. The neutral arbitrator voted with the panel for an award in favor of the party with whom he had done business. Thereafter, the party that lost the arbitration challenged the award, claiming that the failure of the arbitrator to disclose his significant business relationship with the winning party amounted to "evident partiality," warranting vacatur of the award. A majority of the Court reached the conclusion that vacatur was warranted even though there was no proof of actual bias or partiality on the part of the arbitrator and no proof that the undisclosed connection had any direct impact on the deliberations leading to the award. The mere fact that the relationship had not been disclosed on a timely basis was sufficient to warrant the finding of "evident partiality" and to strike down the award.

The threat of this sort of possible presumption enforces the duty to investigate and disclose. Remember, arbitrators are extremely concerned about having their awards challenged. A vacated award can be a professional death knell.

- **If arbitrators disclose and no party makes a timely objection, the conflict is waived.**

The flip side of the "stick" discussed in the previous section is the "carrot" of absolution. If an arbitrator discloses and no one makes a timely objection, the disclosure absolves the arbitrator of concerns about partiality. Basically, a failure to object may constitute a waiver that excuses whatever concerns might have existed based on the disclosed fact.

Of course, parties might also expressly waive a conflict. Going back to my recent experience consulting on an arbitration, the arbitrator who serves as an adjunct at my law school immediately disclosed the potential conflict when she learned about its existence. Both parties expressly waived the conflict without any hesitation. As a result, neither could later use that conflict as a basis for seeking vacatur of any award.

• **If arbitrators disclose and a party objects, the arbitrators determine if they should continue with the appointment, but the issue is preserved for a court to reconsider at the enforcement stage.**

Even if disclosure results in a party objecting that an arbitrator might be partial, the arbitrator or the panel may consider what happens next. The arbitrators might decide that the alleged conflict does not amount to something serious enough to warrant recusal.

The party's objection, however, preserves the issue for a court to consider at the end of the process, during the review and enforcement stage. So, in practice, most arbitrators voluntarily withdraw from an appointment if a party objects to their impartiality.

C. *Procedural Misconduct*

Parties may give up their "day in court" when they agree to arbitrate, but they still have a reasonable right to be heard. FAA § 10(a)(3) permits courts to vacate an arbitration award where "the arbitrators were guilty of misconduct in refusing to postpone the hearing, upon sufficient cause shown, or in refusing to hear evidence pertinent and material to the controversy; or of any other misbehavior by which the rights of any party have been prejudiced." *See also* RUAA § 23 (same). This provision has been summarized by courts as requiring arbitrators to provide the parties with a "fundamentally fair hearing."[3]

Misconduct could occur because an arbitrator fails to postpone a hearing for cause or refuses to hear pertinent and material evidence. But in practice, these issues come up infrequently. First, arbitrators enjoy broad discretion regarding the management of hearings and the receipt of evidence under the law of arbitration. Standard arbitration rules reinforce that discretion. Parties are not entitled to a perfect process but only a reasonable one. Second, and perhaps more importantly, arbitrators tend to err on the side of allowing all evidence to be heard. Arbitrators have strong professional incentives to make sure that their awards are enforceable, and one of the easiest ways to do this is by allowing all evidence to be considered. A court might vacate an award because an arbitrator excluded evidence, but no court will vacate an award because an arbitrator allowed irrelevant evidence to be used in a hearing.

In the extraordinary case where procedural misconduct serves as the basis for vacating an award, courts tend to find that the arbitrator treated one side significantly better than the other. In other words, an arbitrator gave one party additional or extra opportunity to present its evidence or otherwise be heard.

D. *Excess of Authority*

Arbitrators' power derives from the arbitration agreement. Arbitrators can only do what the parties have said they can.

FAA § 10(a)(4) permits courts to vacate an arbitration award where "the arbitrators exceeded their powers." *See also* RUAA § 23

---

[3]   *See, e.g., Legacy Trading Co., Ltd. v. Hoffman,* 2010 WL 325893, at *3 (10th Cir.2010).

(same). Courts usually vacate awards under this provision in three circumstances:

- **Where there is no valid arbitration agreement, or the agreement does not cover the dispute in question.**

  This circumstance should look familiar. This comes up when a challenge to the enforceability of an arbitration agreement does not get heard in court at the outset of the dispute. As Chapter 6 discussed, challenges to the enforceability of the arbitration agreement might not be heard in court because: (a) parties decide to raise them in front of the arbitrator instead, (b) the separability doctrine pushes contract-related issues to the arbitrator; or (c) the parties included a delegation clause. In all of these circumstances, an arbitrator, rather than a court, will have the first opportunity to decide if a dispute is contractually arbitrable. But the excess-of-authority ground for reviewing arbitral awards always allows a court another opportunity to consider these questions. If no arbitration agreement exists, then everything an arbitrator does exceeds her authority. She doesn't have any!

- **Where the arbitrators somehow alter the parties' contractual obligations.**

  The second situation is harder to pin down. Some courts will vacate an award if the arbitrator's decision is not grounded on the agreement of the parties. While courts should not review the merits of an arbitrator's decision, sometimes courts will look to see if the arbitral award "draws its essence from the agreement."

The Supreme Court has explained it this way:

> *A party seeking relief under [§ 10(a)(4)] bears a heavy burden. It is not enough to show that the arbitrator committed an error—or even a serious error. Because the parties bargained for the arbitrator's construction of their agreement, an arbitral decision even arguably construing or applying the contract must stand, regardless of a court's view of its (de)merits. Only if the arbitrator acts outside the scope of his contractually delegated authority—issuing an award that simply reflects his own notions of economic justice rather than drawing its essence from the contract—may a court overturn his determination. So the sole question for us is whether the arbitrator (even arguably) interpreted the parties' contract, not whether he got its meaning right or wrong.*

Oxford Health Plans LLC v. Sutter, 133 S.Ct. 2064, 2068 (2013) *(quotations and citations omitted).*

What courts mean by this is that the award needs to be based on a plausible interpretation of the container contract. If an arbitrator fails to give a plausible reading to the container contract, courts may conclude that the arbitrator has not done the job assigned to her.

- **Where the arbitrators fail to meet the obligations that parties have established for them in the arbitration contract.**

The third situation constitutes a sort of catch-all. Arbitration amounts to a self-governance process where parties hire the arbitrator as their agent to interpret and apply their contract. Parties can impose clear limits or requirements on arbitrators. Arbitrators must abide by those limits or requirements.

For instance, the parties could restrict the range of remedies that arbitrators can award, say capping any award at $250,000. If an arbitrator nevertheless awards $400,000, the losing party may challenge the award on the basis that it exceeded the authority of the arbitrator. Or the parties might say that the arbitrator must provide written reasons justifying and explaining any award. If the arbitrator fails to provide those written reasons with an award, a party could seek to vacate it for failing to abide by the authority provided in the arbitral contract.

E. *Manifest Disregard of the Law*

Manifest disregard of the law constitutes a non-statutory ground of review that many federal and state courts continue to use. It's non-statutory in that it does not appear in the text of the FAA or the RUAA.

The phrase "manifest disregard" originated in *Wilko v. Swan*. *Wilko*, briefly discussed in Chapter 3, was decided prior to the U.S. Supreme Court's love affair with arbitration. Indeed, *Wilko* was eventually overruled. The real legacy of *Wilko*, however, is manifest disregard of the law. In the case, the Court stated that "the interpretations of the law by the arbitrators in contrast to *manifest disregard* are not subject, in the federal courts, to judicial review for error in interpretation" (emphasis added). Lower courts have relied on this language to fashion the modern manifest disregard of the law doctrine.

Before considering the meaning of the doctrine, it's important to note that grave doubt and confusion surrounds it. The confusion stems from the U.S. Supreme Court itself. The Court in *Hall Street Associates, L.L.C. v. Mattel, Inc.*, held that the FAA's four grounds for vacatur are "exclusive." These provisions substantiate

> a national policy favoring arbitration with just the limited review needed to maintain arbitration's essential virtue of resolving disputes straightaway. Any other reading opens the door to the full-bore legal and evidentiary appeals that can render informal arbitration merely a prelude to a more cumbersome and time-consuming judicial review process and bring arbitration theory to grief in post-arbitration process.

This language indicated that manifest disregard no longer constituted an independent basis for review of awards. But later in the decision, the Court declined to decide what its holding meant for the existence of manifest disregard. Two years later, the Court doubled down on the uncertainty, declaring "We do not decide whether 'manifest disregard' survives our decision in *Hall Street* as an independent ground for review or judicial gloss on the enumerated grounds for vacatur set forth [in FAA] . . ."[4]

Lower courts frankly don't know what to do with this state of affairs.

Making matters worse, the doctrine has a potentially critical function to play in modern arbitration law. When arbitration was limited to commercial disputes centered on contracts, there was little need to be worried about whether arbitrators followed the law. In fact, as you've seen, one of the potential advantages of

---

[4]   *Stolt-Nielsen SA v. Animal Feeds Int'l Corp.*, 130 S. Ct. 1758, 1768 n.3. (2010).

arbitration can be that arbitrators are empowered to resolve disputes using standards other than law, including trade usages or industry standards.   That flexibility pairs well with contract or commercial disputes where substantive law is composed mostly of default rules anyway.   Parties are generally free to alter or tailor substantive rules that they want to govern their relationship, so there's no analytically sound reason to prevent them from contracting for the process used to determine their substantive rights.

But when arbitration gets used to resolve disputes involving statutory rights or other mandatory bodies of law, something has to prevent arbitrators from blatantly disregarding those rights or bodies of law.   For instance, imagine an employee who has committed to have any and all disputes with her employer resolved by arbitration.   She brings a claim against her employer in arbitration alleging that she has been discriminated against on the basis of her race.   The arbitrator cannot be free to disregard the employee's civil rights and rely on trade usages or industry standards to conclude that the employee has no damages.   That would effectively mean that the employee abandoned her civil rights by choosing arbitration!

Given the confusion over the state of the doctrine and the practical need to make sure that arbitrators are not completely ignoring fundamental rights, manifest disregard continues to have some role to play in the law of arbitration.

Unfortunately, the precise contours of what the doctrine means are almost as uncertain as its existence.   At this point, however, many courts require the party seeking to vacate an award establish that:

> (1)   the arbitrator ignored law that was well defined, explicit, and clearly applicable; and

(2)   the arbitrator appreciated the existence of this law and refused to apply it.

Those elements are obviously difficult to establish. The reason for the stringency of the standard is that manifest disregard could become a means of second guessing the merits decisions of arbitrators.   As we've seen, merits review of awards would undermine the efficacy of the arbitral process. On the other hand, if manifest disregard becomes too difficult to prove, it cannot operate to prevent wholesale depravations of civil rights.

At this point in history, for good or for bad, few cases are vacated on the basis of manifest disregard.

3.   Judicial Modification of Awards

Courts have extremely limited power to fix minor mistakes in arbitral awards.   FAA § 11 and RUAA § 24 make possible the enforcement of awards containing non-substantive errors. At the request of one of the parties, courts have the power to modify or correct awards for inadvertent technical errors that might otherwise preclude enforcement. The errors in question must be "evident" and unrelated to the merits of the award.

The sort of errors that can be corrected are things like a missing digit from a date or a misspelling of a name.

4.   The Frontiers of Judicial Review

With the exception of manifest disregard of the law, federal law governing enforcement and review of arbitral awards seems reasonably stable.   In addition to the continuing debates about manifest disregard, the cutting edge of judicial review focuses on the interface between state and federal law.

As you know from Chapter 4, the FAA § 2 has preemptive force, and other sections of the FAA, like §§ 3 and 4, may have *de facto* preemptive force. But some sections of the FAA may not preempt state law. In particular, FAA §§ 9, 10, and 11 probably do not directly apply in state courts, and they may not be preemptive in spirit. That, at least, is a fair reading of the dicta in *Hall Street*. As Chapter 4 briefly discussed, *Hall Street* seemed to suggest that the FAA does not prevent state law adding some grounds for vacatur beyond those in FAA § 10. In contrast, however, some federal courts before *Hall Street* held that the FAA preempts state grounds not found in federal law.

Practically, it often doesn't matter. Most state laws of arbitration provide for functionally equivalent standards of judicial review as the FAA. For instance, RUAA § 23 maps onto FAA § 10 with no substantive differences. The interesting and open question, though, is whether state laws must follow the FAA. In other words, could states provide for grounds for judicial review of arbitral awards that are different—more searching or less searching—than federal law?

To date, definitive answers have not been provided by the U.S. Supreme Court. Several states have taken *Hall Street*'s dicta to heart and have created—through statute or through their highest courts—grounds for reviewing arbitral awards that add to the grounds provided in FAA § 10. In essence, a few states have been regulating the backend of the arbitral process. Given that states cannot regulate arbitration on the front end, many commentators are skeptical that, if pushed too far, these sorts of state standards for reviewing and enforcing arbitral awards may be preempted. Unless and until the U.S. Supreme Court speaks, however, at least some possibility of state regulation of arbitral review standards exists.

CHAPTER 8

Is Arbitration Fair?: Consumers, Employees, and Other Disparate Parties

In some situations, arbitration starts to look less like a choice and more like an unavoidable requirement of being employed or buying consumer goods or services.

Critics use the terms "mandatory arbitration" or "forced arbitration" to describe mass-market arbitration agreements requiring aggrieved individuals to resolve their disputes in an arbitral process chosen by the commercial party involved. That terminology may be evocative, but it can also be misleading. All arbitration is "mandatory" or "forced" in the sense that if parties promise to use it, they can then be compelled to follow through on their promises. Nevertheless, pre-dispute arbitration agreements in the consumer, patient, and employee context—what we'll call the disparate party context—remove individuals' access to courts and replace it with what many regard as an inferior, stingier form of arbitral justice, stripped of the threat of class actions. These agreements frequently appear in boilerplate. The nature of these standardized terms and conditions gives the individual little or no room to negotiate. The individual's only options are to accept the terms proposed by the commercial party or walk away from the transaction.

The use of arbitration in the disparate party context is relatively new. For many years, even after the passage of the FAA in 1925, arbitration served as a forum for resolution of primarily commercial disputes. The rule and spirit of *Wilko v. Swan*, a 1953 U.S. Supreme Court decision holding that arbitration was not available for the resolution of at least some statutory rights, limited the feasibility of arbitration between disparate parties.

Throughout the 1980s and 90s, the Court systematically dismantled *Wilko* and it's reasoning, expanding the substantive scope of arbitration. We've talked about this as the erosion of subject matter limitations on arbitrability. The Court concluded that virtually all civil issues can be resolved in arbitration.

This jurisprudential shift presented an opportunity for commercial parties to keep consumers', patients', and workers' claims out of court—and away from jury trial. Accordingly, corporate counsel soon began to include arbitration clauses in an expanding range of adhesive contracts. The result was that arbitration embraced more disputants and different types of relationships between them. Arbitration no longer applied just to relatively evenly-matched commercial parties. It began to apply to *unequally* situated individuals versus business entities.

This Chapter considers this watershed change and its consequences. It begins by identifying the patterns of objections raised to disparate party arbitration, and some of the counterarguments. The Chapter then turns to the critical issue of class action waivers before evaluating the policing role of the doctrine of unconscionability.

1. A Primer on a Few Key Public Policy Issues Surrounding Disparate Party Arbitration

In the past two decades, arbitration has become a feature of everyday life. Most of us are parties to dozens of arbitration agreements, whether we know it or not. These sorts of arbitration agreements implicate at least three different sets of fairness concerns:

- **Concerns about formation of the arbitration agreement.** The covert nature of many mass-market arbitration agreements suggests that individuals are not really choosing arbitration. Individuals who are unaware of the existence of an arbitration provision, or who have no idea what arbitration entails, cannot be making informed or thoughtful decisions about the tradeoffs involved.

- **Concerns about the fairness of the arbitral process itself.** The independence and impartiality of decision makers may be jeopardized in disparate party arbitration, because arbitrators have systematic incentives to favor the stronger party. Additionally, the stronger party has the power to skew specific procedures used in the arbitral process in its favor. These procedures could include where and when the arbitration will take place, the costs of the forum and arbitrators, the time frame of the arbitration, the availability of class actions, and access to discovery, among other things.

- **Concerns about the outcomes in arbitration.** Arbitrators may reach decisions that are different and less favorable to individuals, in predictable and consistent ways. For instance, damages awards may be lower, and punitive damages may be assessed less frequently. Moreover, arbitration awards may be private or even confidential and thus unable to be used as precedents for future individuals in similar fights. And, of course, arbitration awards are not appealable on the merits, limiting the ability of individuals to correct any factual or legal inaccuracies.

A. *Concerns About Formation of the Arbitration Agreement*

Arbitration agreements between disparate parties might not really count as contracts at all.

For instance, Uber drivers and riders have recently filed a wave of class actions challenging the ridesharing service's labor and service practices. In its defense, Uber has turned to its boilerplate. The company has argued that the plaintiffs agreed to its software license and online services agreement by accessing its smartphone application—which they needed to do in order to pick up passengers or get a ride. The agreement included an arbitration clause. When drivers or riders assented to the container license and services agreement, Uber has claimed that they also assented to an arbitration clause. That arbitration clause included a provision saying that drivers were waiving their right to bring a class action.

Courts have divided over whether riders really agreed to Uber's arbitration clause and class action wavier. Most recently, the First Circuit Court of Appeals, applying Massachusetts contract law, concluded that riders were not reasonably notified of the terms of the agreement. Accordingly, there was no opportunity for mutual assent to those terms.[1] Without mutual assent, no contract can

---

[1]   *Cullinane v. Uber Techs., Inc.*, 893 F.3d 53, 61 (1st Cir. 2018).

exist. On the other hand, the Second Circuit Court of Appeals, applying California contract law, reached the exact opposite conclusion, finding that "the design of the screen and language used render the notice provided reasonable as a matter of California law."[2] Accordingly, it held that riders were bound to arbitrate their claims.

Tempting as it might be to chalk the difference in outcomes up to nuances in Massachusetts and California law, no material differences exist. Both states require virtually identical showings for mutual assent. The difference, it seems, turns on how judges view the conspicuousness of boilerplate terms. But if judges, who are by definition experts in the law, can view identical facts in such radically contrasting ways, how is anyone else to understand what the rules for mutual assent to boilerplate are?

This question has been at the core of an important and vigorous academic debate raging for the past couple of decades. Most courts, including the U.S. Supreme Court, have concluded that, despite their unilateral character, adhesive agreements are commonly enforceable as contracts, so long as the recipient was reasonably put on notice of the existence of the terms. As the Uber cases indicate, however, a great deal of disagreement over what counts as reasonable notice persists. Moreover, some commentators believe that the logic of the reasonable notice rule rests on a shaky foundation. It constitutes a gerrymandering of the term "agreement" or "consent." Being put on notice of something doesn't equate to agreeing to that something.

Compare the hypothetical consent suggested by the reasonable notice approach to the idea of a contract that law students learn in their first year. In an ideal world, a contract results from parties choosing to give up an entitlement or property interest in order to

---

[2]   *Meyer v. Uber Techs., Inc.*, 868 F.3d 66, 78 (2d Cir. 2017).

get something they value more highly in exchange. Choice matters. It is the voluntariness of the exchange that provides a moral foundation for contract law. Autonomous individuals should be free to form, revise and pursue their own plans and conceptions of what it means to live a fulfilling and meaningful life. Parties are free to make bad exchanges, so long as they are really choosing to make them. Contract law doesn't protect parties from lousy deals, but it generally prevents coerced or forced ones.

Boilerplate terms and conditions that individuals never see or read or understand chafe against this ideal. It's difficult to conceive of individuals as "agreeing" or "choosing" terms they don't know about or understand. It's even more difficult to believe that individuals are voluntarily opting to give up their rights in exchange for something else. Instead, boilerplate starts to look and feel a lot like a non-consensual taking of entitlements or property interests. The notion that hypothetical consent can be implied so long as an individual had reasonable notice of the boilerplate doesn't really provide much comfort.

For our purposes, it's important to see that these sorts of arguments about the quality of assent are significant to arbitration agreements, but they are not limited to them. In fact, individuals are held to a lot of other standardized terms and conditions that are arguably much more detrimental than arbitration. Forced arbitration may be one type of concerning boilerplate, but it is far from the only term that could disproportionately benefit commercial parties.

It's also worth briefly discussing the counterarguments.

Most counterarguments focus on the fact that boilerplate terms and conditions result in lower costs for individuals (or, in the case of employment contracts, higher pay). Individuals, these arguments suggest, prefer lower prices (or higher wages). Like default rules, boilerplate economizes on process costs by focusing on what most people want most of the time.

Everyone seems to agree that boilerplate provisions likely reduce costs to commercial parties. That, after all, is why commercial parties want to include such provisions. What commercial parties do with the savings, however, remains a contested issue. Some commentators suggest that the savings could be pocketed by the commercial parties rather than passed on to individuals. Others maintain that the nature of mass market transactions requires commercial parties to pass these savings on, at least in the long run.

The logic of the second line of thinking is that an unscrupulous commercial party could theoretically steal cost-savings from other product or service attributes as well. If we conceive of boilerplate as just another product attribute—like the quality of microprocessor used in a smartphone or the materials used to construct a brake pad on a car—it becomes easier to see that mass-market transactions often have attributes that many individuals do not know about or understand. When buying a smartphone, most consumers don't have the foggiest idea about subtle differences in microprocessors. Similarly, most car buyers have little or no understanding of differences in materials used to construct brake pads. Buyers are, instead, agreeing to the general gist of the transaction and leaving the details to the sellers. Sellers wanting to bilk consumers could overcharge for lower quality microprocessors or brake pads and keep the savings as profits. But the market tends to discipline such sellers, at least in the long run.

Mass markets benefit from large groups of individuals who have varying degrees of knowledge or experience. Commercial parties cannot distinguish between sophisticated individuals who might understand a particular product attribute and more typical individuals who do not understand that attribute. As long as there are enough sophisticated individuals, or as long as sophisticated individuals can share their experiences with enough typical individuals, commercial parties must remain reasonably honest or be chased out of business.

Or so goes the theory.

Some commentators argue that it doesn't really matter anyway. Even if consumers get lower prices (or employees get higher pay), nothing about boilerplate suggests that individuals chose this benefit in exchange for giving up their right to go to a public court. Accordingly, even if individuals are being compensated, they are being forced to make an exchange, and that feels like private eminent domain—a taking, albeit a compensated one, without voluntary agreement. We don't allow private parties to take another's property unilaterally, even if they pay for it. Theft of your car doesn't become less problematic because the thief leaves you a check for its value. Private eminent domain does not exist.

Ultimately, there are strong arguments on both sides of debates about mutual assent to boilerplate terms and conditions, including arbitration. Again, it's important to understand, for our purposes, that the issues and arguments are not limited to arbitration agreements. Public discourse about boilerplate has sometimes become focused on arbitration. Arbitration has become a sort of stalking horse used to avoid more nuanced conversations about the real complexities of mass market contracting more generally.

Any thoughtful appraisal of arbitration between disparate parties needs to consider that arbitration agreements are merely one out of a number of potentially concerning terms forced onto individuals. Boilerplate contracting, however, does pose serious policy and doctrinal concerns that cannot be brushed aside simply by acknowledging that, to date, most courts have been willing to enforce such contracts when individuals are given reasonable notice.

B. Concerns About the Fairness of the Arbitral Process Itself

Arbitration may offer a number of comparative advantages to litigation in a public court. But when arbitration is unilaterally chosen by the stronger party, those advantages can start to look pretty one-sided.

As discussed in Chapter 2, many of the pros of arbitration may seem like cons from a different perspective. Individuals in disparate party arbitration agreements, however, might be specifically worried about a few features of the arbitral process:

- **Repeat players versus one-shot players**—Individuals might be disadvantaged, or perceive themselves as disadvantaged, because the commercial party who drafted the arbitration provision is a repeat party to arbitrations, familiar with the process and with arbitrators. In contrast, an individual may have only one arbitration in her entire life. That imbalance could make the arbitral process feel like an insider's game. Even if that feeling is not empirically well-founded, perceptions matter when it comes to fairness. Parties will accept a loss more readily if they believe the process was fair.

- **Processes tilted in the commercial parties' favor**—Because the commercial party has drafted the arbitration agreement, it may subtly (and not so subtly) tilt various aspects of the process in its favor, including rights to discovery, the location of the hearing, the confidentiality of the process, and the ability of individuals to aggregate their claims with other individuals.

- **Up-front costs**—Arbitration can be more expensive than public court litigation, at least at the outset. High costs of initiating arbitration and the fees of arbitrators can be daunting. Individuals might be dissuaded from bringing meritorious claims by these costs.

There are a number of retorts to these concerns. Perhaps most importantly, arbitration institutions have actively sought to offset worries about fairness by passing various "due process" protocols. The AAA, for instance, has co-sponsored several national efforts to establish due process standards. Those efforts have resulted in the AAA making changes to its own rules and procedures. They have also inspired the development of analogous rules by some other provider organizations.

One example was the *Due Process Protocol for Mediation and Arbitration of Statutory Disputes Arising Out of the Employment Relationship* (Employment Due Process Protocol), adopted by the AAA and JAMS in the mid-1990s. It aimed to correct for imbalances employment arbitrations by allowing employees to be represented by an attorney, having the employer reimburse the employee for attorney fees, encouraging the use of pretrial discovery, and allowing the arbitrator to provide any type of relief that would be similar to that available in a court proceeding. The Employment Due Process Protocol served as the template for a number of subsequent similar efforts in other disparate party contexts. At this point, numerous due process protocols or similar mechanisms exist.

Some commentators remain skeptical, however, of these sorts of self-regulating efforts. These due process protocols do not have the force of law and are, thus, at bottom voluntary undertakings.

Without some mandatory protections, some commentators argue, self-regulation merely masks fairness problems.

C. *Concerns About the Outcomes in Arbitration*

Arbitration substitutes for courts. But sometimes the outcomes in arbitration might not be perceived as equal to what individuals would have received in public court.

In particular, the arbitral process may result in individuals getting lower damages awards. A commercial party might want to arbitrate precisely because it believes that arbitrators will be less emotional or extreme than courts or juries when awarding damages. As industry experts, arbitrators may be more dispassionate and potentially even biased in favor of the industry. Additionally, arbitrators might be less inclined to award punitive or exemplary damages.

And awards can be private or even confidential, limiting the ability of individuals to help other similarly situated people who have suffered similar wrongs at the hands of the same commercial party. Moreover, arbitration, of course, is final and binding with no merits appeals available.

These outcome-based concerns raise important empirical questions. At present, limited data exists to validate them, particularly with respect to the damages awarded in arbitrations.

Regardless of the empirical realities, these outcome-based concerns really only have bite if, in fact, parties are not choosing arbitration in the first instance. No one thinks that arbitration amounts to a substantively equivalent process to public court litigation. But if parties are voluntarily trading pros and cons of the processes, freedom of contract allows them to do so, even if the results are bad. Freedom of contract includes the freedom to make a bad deal. The trouble, as the concerns about formation of arbitration agreements highlights, is that individuals may not really be making these sorts of tradeoff decisions. If parties are not really choosing arbitration, then outcome-based concerns take on greater significance.

2. Class Action Waivers

Perhaps the most heated disagreements over arbitration center on so-called class action waivers.

Essentially, the U.S. Supreme Court has determined that the FAA empowers commercial parties not only to include arbitration clauses in their boilerplate contracts, but also to prohibit individuals from aggregating their claims with other people. A chorus of critics has heralded this jurisprudential change as one of the most profound shifts in legal history.

Let's look at its evolution.

As U.S. Supreme Court jurisprudence was becoming more protective of consumer and employment arbitration contracts, forcing individuals to arbitrate claims rather than take them to court, consumer class actions were also on the rise. For commercial parties, class actions pose much greater financial risk than individual lawsuits, whether litigated or arbitrated. Class actions allow many similarly situated parties to aggregate their claims together. Pooled claims can create tremendous settlement pressure.

Think of it this way: imagine that Belinda Customer alleges that Big Bank has taken $1 a month out of her checking account without authorization for ten years. Individually, she's only suffered $120 dollars of harm. But if she can find 1,000,000 similarly situated customers of Big Bank and aggregate her claims with theirs, the total damages could now be upwards of $120 million. That may seem perfectly acceptable if we assume that Big Bank has done something wrong. After all, Big Bank should not be allowed to cheat its customers.

But what if Belinda's theory that this charge was unauthorized rests on a dubious legal foundation. What if every banking expert agrees that there's only a 3% chance that Belinda can or should prevail after a trial. So, there's a 97% chance that this is a losing case. The trouble is that Big Bank, if it's a rational actor, should still settle the dispute for at least $3.6 million plus whatever it would expect to spend on its own attorneys to defend the case through trial. That settlement amount represents the expected cost of the lawsuit to Big Bank.[3]

Class actions, in short, may incentivize entrepreneurial litigators to bring questionable claims against commercial parties because the prospect of huge losses can extract quick settlements. Many class actions, after all, involve contingency fee arrangements, so Belinda's attorneys could stand to earn 35-40%, or more, of the total settlement—at least $1.26-1.44 million.   The 1,000,000 individuals allegedly harmed by Big Bank, meanwhile, would each get checks for less than $2.

Of course, this skeptical view of class actions has to be counterbalanced by the fact that without them, individuals like Belinda may have no meaningful opportunity to protect themselves from predatory businesses. If, in fact, Big Bank has engaged in a systematic scheme to defraud its customers for small amounts, it has made millions of dollars unlawfully. What's worse, it's done so while insulating itself from any liability from any individual. Each individual who has been defrauded hasn't lost enough to justify doing anything about it. Aggregative processes might be the only way to hold Big Bank accountable.

---

[3] $120 million multiplied by the probability of losing (3%) plus the costs of fighting.

Whatever one thinks of the controversial debates regarding class actions, commercial parties saw the Supreme Court's love of arbitration as an opportunity to avoid them entirely. Commercial parties began including bars to class actions in mandatory pre-dispute arbitration clauses. In other words, they began mandating that individuals arbitrate any and all disputes and do so on their own.

Initial judicial response to these clauses varied, with some courts allowing arbitrators to decide whether a clause contemplated class arbitration. Other courts voided the bars against class actions using the doctrine of unconscionability. For instance, in *Discover Bank v. Superior Court*, the California Supreme Court said:

> We do not hold that all class action waivers are necessarily unconscionable. But when the waiver is found in a consumer contract of adhesion in a setting in which disputes between the contracting parties predictably involve small amounts of damages, and when it is alleged that the party with the superior bargaining power has carried out a scheme to deliberately cheat large numbers of consumers out of individually small sums of money, then, at least to the extent the obligation at issue is governed by California law, the waiver becomes in practice the exemption of the party "from responsibility for [its] own fraud, or willful injury to the person or property of another." (Civ. Code, § 1668.) Under these circumstances, such waivers are unconscionable under California law and should not be enforced.[4]

In 2011, the U.S. Supreme Court, ended the debate. In *AT&T Mobility v. Concepcion*, it held that the *Discover Bank* rule was preempted by the FAA.[5] According to the Court, "[t]he overarching

---

[4]　30 Cal.Rptr.3d 76, 87 (Cal. 2005).
[5]　563 U.S. 333 (2011).

purpose of the FAA, evident in the text of §§ 2, 3, and 4, is to ensure the enforcement of arbitration agreements according to their terms so as to facilitate streamlined proceedings."[6] In the Court's view, arbitration has certain fundamental attributes that render it a more streamlined process than litigation in a public court. The FAA protects the parties' right to choose these more streamlined processes. States cannot regulate the recourse to arbitration, and requiring parties to consent to class actions in arbitration would interfere with the parties' freedom of choice.

Parties may, if they want, authorize class actions in arbitration, but the holding of *Concepcion* is that parties are free to preclude class actions as well.

In 2013, the Court added that class action waivers in arbitration agreements are enforceable even if, as a consequence, parties cannot effectively vindicate their rights. In *American Express Co. v. Italian Colors Restaurant*, a class of small businesses brought antitrust claims against American Express.[7] The small business plaintiffs argued that, without aggregative process, they would be prevented from vindicating their rights. To prove an antitrust claim of the sort that they were alleging, the plaintiffs needed an expert report, which would cost between $200,000 and $1 million. No individual plaintiff's damages, however, exceeded $38,500. The Court found that the fact that it might be too expensive to pursue a statutory claim in individual arbitration was not equivalent to eliminating the right to pursue the remedy. Accordingly, even if practically it would be impossible to vindicate a right without aggregative process, class action waivers are still enforceable as part of arbitral clauses.

---

[6] *Id.* at 334.
[7] 133 S. Ct. 2304 (2013).

Since these cases, the Court has only continued to reinforce its pro-arbitration freedom position, effectively allowing businesses to use arbitration clauses as a shield against class action liability.

3. **Unconscionability and Adhesive Arbitration**

As the previous sections have suggested, there are serious concerns about the fairness of arbitration in the disparate party context.

Courts, however, may intervene to protect individuals from drastically unfair arbitration by striking down specific terms in the arbitration agreement or denying enforcement of the agreement entirely. These sorts of interventions may be rooted in a variety of generally applicable contract law defenses, but the most significant is unconscionability.

Chapter 6 discussed unconscionability in more detail, but it's worth highlighting the fact that the doctrine has been used extensively in the context of disparate party arbitration. Indeed, unconscionability arguments outside of the disparate party context are almost surely doomed to fail. Even with respect to boilerplate contracts of adhesion, unconscionability challenges to arbitration agreements face strong headwinds. That said, courts can and do use the doctrine to police arbitration agreements.

While not exclusive, most successful unconscionability arguments fall into three broad categories:

- **Mutuality of the obligation to arbitrate**—A red flag goes up if only one party has the obligation to arbitrate. Sometimes, a commercial party requires an individual to arbitrate any and all claims but reserves for itself the right go to public courts for claims it may have. The more one-sided the obligation to arbitrate is, the more skeptical courts get.

The best policy for commercial parties is to make the obligation to arbitrate reciprocal. Perfect mutuality may not be required, but courts rightfully scrutinize carveouts in disparate party arbitration agreements. More and more boilerplate arbitration agreements are perfectly mutual in order to avoid this concern.

- **Costs**—Arbitration can be costly, especially at the outset. Mass-market arbitration clauses that impose high costs on individuals may be deemed unconscionable.

  Excessive costs could include not only the costs of the arbitrators or institutional fees, but also costs of traveling to the location where the hearings are to be held. Additionally, arbitration clauses that restrict the right of successful plaintiffs to recover attorneys' fees or punitive damages when they would be available in a public court may be unconscionable.

  Analytically, the costs of arbitration should be concerning only if they exceed by a meaningful margin the costs of litigating in a public court. Some claims may simply not be worth pursuing in any forum.

  The best policy for commercial parties is to pay the costs of the arbitration on behalf of individuals. If commercial parties absorb the costs of the arbitration process, this basis for finding a clause unconscionable disappears.

- **Severe restraints on the process**—Egregious limitations on procedures available in arbitration may be problematic. Although arbitration allows for a broad range of customizations, even facially equal processes may begin to look one-sided in practice if individuals are severely restricted in their ability to obtain evidence or in the timeframe during which they may bring a claim. Additionally, arbitration clauses that impose onerous confidentiality provisions or burdensome limits on choices of arbitrators may be deemed unconscionable.

CHAPTER 9

A Peek at International Commercial Arbitration

When it comes to cross-border business transactions, international commercial arbitration ("ICA") constitutes the principal method of adjudicating disputes. The expansion of ICA parallels the rise of globalization. As businesses have conducted more and more transactions across national borders, the need to address the risks of sometimes conflicting and often opaque regulations among countries has grown. ICA helps parties avoid pitfalls associated with domestic legal systems while efficiently resolving their disputes.

This Chapter provides an overview of ICA. It doesn't aim to give you detailed coverage of any specific issue, but it should help you see the big picture. The Chapter then introduces the New York Convention on enforcement of foreign arbitral awards, and it concludes with a brief consideration of investor-state arbitration.

1. The 10,000 Meter View[1]

In many respects, ICA functions similarly to domestic arbitration. The fundamental characteristics are mostly the same, and the core concepts are virtually identical. Moreover, the pros and cons of ICA are nearly identical, with three additional benefits existing for ICA:

- **Avoiding homecourts.** Parties to international disputes could worry about "hometown" or "homecourt" advantage—concerns about litigating in the other party's national courts. Home courts of one party might be biased in the local party's favor. Additionally, the local party will likely have more ready access to attorneys who are experienced in litigating in those courts.

- **Applying a-national standards of decision.** Parties may want arbitrators to apply a-national or transnational rules of decision instead of otherwise applicable national law. One of the advantages to international commercial arbitration, in fact, can be that arbitrators rely on a more harmonized set of norms and expectations governing international businesses than the law of any particular jurisdiction would provide. Sometimes, parties might even prefer that their dispute be resolved by decision makers applying trade or industry norms or general principles of equity instead of legal rules.

- **Enforceability.** Arbitration awards are more widely and readily enforceable than court judgments.

---

[1]   We're talking about international commercial arbitration, after all. "Feet" is a far too "American" a measure to use for this metaphor.

While offering some unique and valuable advantages, ICA also adds layers of complexity, especially in terms of the regulatory framework in which arbitration takes place.

As with any arbitral process, there can be no ICA without the agreement of the parties. And as with domestic arbitration, the parties may incorporate institutional rules, by reference, into their agreement. Where things get more difficult is in determining what law governs:

- The validity of the arbitration agreement;

- The arbitral process itself; and

- The review and enforcement of arbitral awards.

A. *The Validity of the Arbitration Agreement*

In ICA, the law applicable to determine the validity of the arbitration agreement itself is usually the "law of the seat." This also gets variously referred to as the *lex arbitri*, the *procedural law*, or the *curial law*. Whatever one calls it, the parties will usually choose what nation they want to be the "seat." They can do so directly, by naming the "seat" or indirectly by delegating the choice to an administering arbitration institution. The seat's domestic arbitration law will govern the formation, validity and enforceability of the arbitration agreement. In some cases, a nation may have a separate domestic law dedicated to ICA, in which case that law would apply.

Most national laws of arbitration function similarly to U.S. domestic arbitration law. Most other nations, however, have arbitration laws that are articulated in a more comprehensive statute than the FAA. For instance, many countries have enacted a version of the UNCITRAL Model Law on International Commercial Arbitration. The model law represents a thoroughly modern approach to arbitral regulation.

In whatever form it takes, domestic law must implement certain ICA policies, at least for countries that have agreed to the Convention on Recognition and Enforcement of Foreign Arbitral Awards, commonly referred to simply as the New York Convention.[2] Specifically, contracting countries must make sure that their domestic arbitration laws

> recognize an agreement in writing under which the parties undertake to submit to arbitration all or any differences which have arisen or which may arise between them in respect of a defined legal relationship, whether contractual or not, concerning a subject matter capable of settlement by arbitration.[3]

As is true in domestic arbitration, the remedy for breach of a valid ICA agreement, under the New York Convention, is to stay any pending litigation and refer the parties to arbitration.[4]

A few things are important to note about the "law of the seat":

- **The seat of arbitration usually corresponds to the place where the arbitral hearing takes place.**

  Usually, the seat of the arbitration is the location of the arbitral hearing. The "law of the seat" concept was historically geographical in nature. Sovereignty and the power of a country to have its laws applied were, for much of history, bounded by national borders. In that context, it makes sense to find that the law governing the arbitration should be the law where the arbitration physically occurs.

---

[2] In the U.S., the New York Convention has been appended to the FAA. *See* 9 U.S.C. § 201 *et. seq.*

[3] New York Convention, art. II(1).

[4] *See id.* art. II(3).

Modern approaches to law, however, have generally become far less territorial in nature. As the territorialist grip on international law eroded, courts began to recognize that parties could agree on a "law of the seat" that differs from the physical location of the hearing. There's no necessary connection between where the arbitration hearing takes place and the law applied to the arbitration.

- **Some commentators have advocated for a "delocalized" or "a-national" approach to the *lex arbitri*.**

  While mostly beyond the scope of our short and happy project, you should know that there have been a number of impassioned arguments in favor of the complete delocalization of ICA. The idea's pretty simple: ICA should not be troubled with the law of the place where the arbitration happens to be "seated." After all, as the previous section noted, there's no logical or necessary connection between the physical location of the arbitration hearing and the abstracted notion of what law governs the arbitration process.

  Delocalization advocates simply extend this logic one step further and say that no law is needed to deal with front end issues—the validity and enforceability of the arbitral agreement—or the arbitral process. The only necessary role for arbitration law, delocalization advocates have argued, is during the review and enforcement stage.

  Delocalization arguments peaked in the 1980s and then tapered off. But a couple of recent trends suggest that at least some of the spirit of delocalization might be making a comeback. Perhaps most pertinently, online arbitrations present serious challenges to any territorialist approach to applicable law. Where does an online arbitration hearing "take place?" To date, the primary answer is that the "law of the seat" can be any jurisdiction that the parties choose, regardless of whether they or the arbitration ever has any connection with that jurisdiction. Not surprisingly, some nations are reluctant to give court access to non-citizens who are doing nothing in, spending no money in, and effectively disconnected from the nation.

- **Things can get messy when the parties choose a substantive law to govern the container contract that differs from the *lex arbitri*.**

    Generally, the *lex arbitri* will govern whether an arbitration agreement is valid and enforceable. But problems can arise if the parties choose a substantive law to apply to the container contract that provides different standards of mutual assent or different defenses to contract formation than the *lex arbitri* applies to arbitration agreements.

    For instance, imagine that Old Iron Brewing, Co., a U.S. business, enters into a distribution agreement containing an arbitral clause with a distributor based out of Germany, Wurst Distribution. The parties select country G as the "seat" of their arbitration. They also select the substantive law of country F to apply to the distribution agreement. What happens if the arbitral clause would not be valid under the arbitral law of country G because of a lack of mutual assent—let's assume a missing signature or other formality. But mutual assent does not require this formality under the law of country F. Is the arbitration agreement "valid" or not?

The answer will usually depend on what the arbitration law of country G says. Some countries—Switzerland, for instance—take an expansive view and provide that the arbitration agreement will be valid if it either complies with local law or "if it complies with the requirements of the . . . law governing the object of the dispute, and, in particular, the law applicable to the principle contract." If Swiss law were applied to the situation between Old Iron and Wurst, the arbitration agreement would be valid.

The UNCITRAL Model Law provides that the parties may select a specific law to govern the validity of the arbitration agreement that differs from the law of the seat. If they do not specifically choose such a law, however, the strong implication is that the validity will be determined by the law of the seat. Under the Model Law, the arbitration agreement between Old Iron and Wurst would probably not be valid.

Finally, some jurisdictions clearly conclude that the law of the seat should govern all issues related to the validity of the arbitration agreement. Under this approach, the arbitration agreement between Old Iron and Wurst would not be valid.

- **The law of the seat governs issues of arbitrability.**

    As with domestic arbitrations, arbitrators must have jurisdiction to render an award. This means, in the parlance of arbitration law, that the arbitrators must have arbitrability. As discussed in Chapters 3 and 7, arbitrability divides into questions of subject matter arbitrability and contractual arbitrability. The law of the seat governs both branches.

    In the United States, almost all civil subjects are arbitrable, so that branch tends to be of limited importance. Internationally, however, many countries provide more rigorous regulation of the subjects that can be sent to arbitration. That issue can be of paramount importance in selecting a seat for the arbitration.

B.   *The Arbitral Process*

The law governing the arbitral process is almost always simply the law of the seat. Few issues arise with respect to this part of the process.

As you'll recall from Chapter 4, arbitration laws governing the process are mostly default rules or rules that aid the arbitral process. That's true in ICA as well as domestically. Another way of saying this is to say that the arbitral process gets regulated primarily by the agreement of the parties, including through any institutional rules that the parties have incorporated by reference into their agreement. Arbitration law provides default rules that apply to the extent that the parties have not addressed an issue or have not altered the default. Additionally, arbitration law provides various mechanisms to support the arbitral process.

The details of what defaults exist or what supporting rules are provided by arbitration laws differs depending on what *lex arbitri* the parties choose.

C. *The Review and Enforcement of Arbitral Awards*

Perhaps more than with domestic arbitrations, parties frequently comply with ICA awards. Accordingly, there's often no need to go to a court to enforce the award.

When a prevailing party needs court help, however, the good news is that it's almost always a relatively straight-forward process to get an ICA award confirmed.

The New York Convention exists primarily for this very purpose. The New York Convention requires courts of contracting states to recognize and enforce both arbitration agreements and arbitration awards in a predictable fashion. A vast majority of countries around the world are contracting states, which means that parties can be confident that if they prevail in an arbitration, they will be able to obtain a remedy.

2. The New York Convention Overview

The New York Convention has made ICA viable. It does two fundamental things: (1) it assures that the domestic law of contracting states enforces ICA agreements, as discussed in the previous section; and (2) it provides for the recognition and enforcement of ICA awards in contracting states.

With respect to the second function, "recognition" means that the contracting state acknowledges that the award is valid and binding, and thereby gives it a preclusive effect with respect to the matters determined in the award. "Enforcement," in contrast, usually refers to the process by which an ICA award gets reduced to a court judgment that can, in turn, be enforced through state-sanctioned means. From here on out, we'll just talk about these as the same thing, under the umbrella of enforcement, but you should understand that they can be technically independent concepts.

Two primary issues come up with respect to enforcement under the New York Convention:

- **Does the Convention apply?** The Convention was intended to apply to international arbitral awards, but it also permits enforcement of nondomestic awards. In the United States, the award must relate to a commercial dispute.

- **Are there any grounds for non-enforcement of the award?** The Convention provides seven defenses to enforcement of an award.

A. Does the Convention Apply?

The New York Convention centers on international arbitration awards. It also permits, however, enforcement of awards considered "nondomestic" by the enforcing jurisdiction.

The term "domestic" is not defined in the Convention, so each contracting state may define the term. In the United States, for instance, an award is nondomestic, even if between citizens of the United States, if the "relationship involves property located abroad, envisages performance of enforcement abroad, or has some other reasonable relation with one or more foreign states."[5] In many other countries, in contrast, only awards rendered in a foreign jurisdiction qualify as "nondomestic."

In addition to this scope issue, contracting states may make two reservations to the Convention. The first focuses on reciprocity: a contracting state can provide that it will apply the

---

[5]   9 U.S.C. § 202.

Convention only to awards that are made in the territory of another contracting state. This reservation has been adopted by approximately half of the contracting states. The United States has not made this reservation.

The second limits the Convention's application to "commercial" disputes. Nearly 50 states have made this reservation, including the United States. Because the term "commercial" is not defined, the law of the enforcing jurisdiction determines what is commercial. In general, however, criminal matters and family matters—including divorce, custody, and adoption, as well as wills and trusts—are not considered "commercial."

B. Are There Any Grounds for Non-Enforcement of the Award?

A losing party might oppose enforcement of the award in the contacting state where enforcement is sought. The Convention provides only a limited number of defenses to enforcement, and these are narrowly construed. Courts tend to enforce arbitral awards under the Convention without second guessing arbitrators.

i. Incapacity and Invalidity

An award might not be enforced because the parties did not have capacity to enter into the agreement to arbitration agreement or because the arbitration agreement was invalid.[6] Both issues will be resolved under the law chosen by the parties, or, if no such law was chosen, the law where the arbitration took place.

Incapacity issues could involve things like the actual and apparent authority of agents, the relationships between subsidiary companies and parent companies, or sovereign immunity for states

---

[6] *Id.* art. V(1)(a).

or state-owned enterprises. Invalidity issues focus on questions of contractual or subject matter arbitrability.

ii. Lack of Notice or Fairness

Parties have a right to be provided with notice of the appointment of the arbitrator and of the arbitral proceedings. Additionally, parties must be given a reasonable opportunity to present their cases. These issues should look familiar, as they amount to the minimal requirements of procedural due process. They are also protected, at least to some degree, by FAA § 10's requirement that there be no procedural misconduct by arbitrators.

The idea is that if minimal requirements are not satisfied, a court may deny enforcement of an arbitral award under the New York Convention, just as it could do under domestic law.[7] But as with domestic protections of minimal due process, courts are reluctant to second guess all but the most egregious violations of due process by arbitrators.

iii. Excess of Authority

An arbitrator's power comes from the consent of the parties, and if the arbitrator exceeds the authority specifically given to her under the parties' arbitration agreement, then the resulting award is not enforceable under the Convention.[8] Again, this should look quite familiar. This defense parallels the similar defense in the FAA.

iv. The Tribunal or the Procedure Was Not Consistent with the Parties' Agreement

If the composition of the tribunal or the processes used in the arbitration do not match the parties' agreement, then a court may

---

[7] *Id.* art. V(1)(b).

[8] *Id.* art. V(1)(c).

refuse to enforce an award.[9] This provision rarely gets used by courts.

v.   The Award Is Not Yet Binding or Has Been Vacated

If the integrity of the award has been questioned, either because the award has not yet become binding or because it has been vacated under the law of the seat, a court may refuse to enforce the award.[10] Although the term "binding" is not defined in the Convention, most courts agree that it means that any the period for merits appeals, if any, under the law of the seat must have expired. As you know, under United States law, there are no merits appeals. Most modern arbitration laws are similar, so this provision of the New York Convention has little practical use.

The second issue is more significant. A disgruntled party could seek to vacate an arbitral award in the country that has been designated as the "seat" of the arbitration. If an award is vacated (sometimes called, in other countries, "set aside" or "annulled"), the New York Convention provides that a court in a contracting state may refuse to enforce the award.

Importantly, the standards for vacating an award are not provided in the Convention. Instead, those standards would be supplied by the law of the seat. For instance, imagine that Big Retailer, based in Canada, and Medium Supplier, located in China, enter into a sales agreement containing an arbitral clause. They designate New York as the "seat" of the arbitration. The parties arbitrate a dispute and Medium Supplier loses. It wants to vacate the award. In the meantime, Big Retailer wants to enforce the award and so goes to a Chinese court to do so. What law would govern Medium Supplier's vacatur? FAA § 10, which is the law of the seat!

---

[9]   *Id.* art. V(1)(d).
[10]   *Id.* art. V(1)(e).

It's also worth highlighting the word "may": a court in a contracting state "may" refuse to enforce an award that has been vacated under the law of the seat. At least theoretically, the use of this permissive term gives courts in the enforcement jurisdiction the discretion to enforce an award even if it has been vacated under the law of the seat. In practice, however, that almost never happens.

vi. The Subject Matter of the Award Is Not Arbitrable

A country's laws may provide that certain types of disputes are not arbitrable. This is what we've discussed as subject matter arbitrability. As you know, in the United States, almost all civil matters are arbitrable. But many countries impose some limits on the subjects that are amenable to resolution in arbitration.

This ground for refusing to enforce an ICA award, however, differs a bit from the previous grounds discussed in that it focuses on the law of the country where enforcement is sought. If the country where the enforcement is sought does not permit arbitration of the subject matter at issue in the award, a court in that country may deny enforcement.[11]

vii. The Award Violates Public Policy

If a court in the country where enforcement of the ICA award is sought finds that enforcing would violate public policy, it can refuse to do so.[12] Most courts have viewed this defense narrowly, refusing to enforce awards only if the forum's most basic notions of morality and justice would be imperiled.

---

[11] *Id.* art. V(2)(a).
[12] *Id.* art. V(2)(b).

3. Intro to Investor-State Arbitration

Investor-state arbitration is a form of binding international dispute resolution. It differs from ICA in that one of the parties involved is a country. Investor-state arbitration permits certain foreign, private investors to file claims against host states. These claims arise when an investor alleges that it has suffered financial loss as a result of violation of one or more standards of treatment set out in a pro-investment treaty or law.

Let's take a moment and unpack this.

Foreign investment has been critical to global economic growth for the past couple of decades. Of course, there are raging debates about the extent and propriety of globalization, but whatever one thinks of the larger discussion, globalization constitutes an important part of business.

The trouble has been that investors considering major capital-intensive projects in host countries worry that they will have their investments seized. Imagine, for instance, that Big Manufacturer wants to invest in building a new $500 million facility in Country Q, a developing nation. Big Manufacturer could be worried that Country Q might outright expropriate—take—the facility, once it's built. More likely, however, is that Country Q might change its regulatory laws in such a way as to reduce greatly the value of the facility. For instance, it could be that Big Manufacturer is interested in building the facility because Country Q imposes minimal property taxes. What happens if Country Q changes its tax laws just as the facility comes on line? That would, at the least, radically change the incentive structure under which Big Manufacturer made its investment decisions.

The bottom line is that investors want assurances that their investments will not be taken over or so undermined by the host country that the investment becomes devalued. They also want a way to resolve disputes with a host country that does not depend on local courts. After all, a foreign investor might be seen by local courts as the big, bad outsider. In a worst-case scenario, the investor might be prevented from suing the host country in a local court altogether by sovereign immunity.

Trying to make investors feel secure, national governments have taken steps to make their laws more investor friendly. Many have adopted investor-protection legislation. In addition, many more have entered into bilateral and multilateral investment treaties.

These treaties vary quite a bit, but they tend to have several common features designed to protect investors, including provisions:

- *Establishing fair and equitable treatment*—This essentially requires host states to provide a reasonably stable investment environment, consistent with investor expectations.

- *Protecting against uncompensated expropriations*— If a government expropriates an investment, it can only do so in a non-discriminatory manner, and the investor must be promptly and adequately compensated. Host state actions that substantially diminish the value of an investment may also be treated as an expropriation.

- *Establishing national treatment*—The host state must generally treat the investor as well as it treats its own nationals.

- *Establishing most favored nation treatment*—The host state must generally treat the investor as well as it treats investors from any other country.

- *Establishing free funds transfer rights*—Funds related to the investment may be freely moved into and out of the host state without extra burdens or requirements.

To vindicate the rights created by these pro-investor treaties, the trend has been to move state-investor disputes into arbitration. To that end, in 1965, the World Bank sponsored a treaty establishing a neutral forum for the resolution of investment disputes between states and nationals of other states. Known as the Washington Convention or the ICSID Convention, the treaty created an organization to deal with investment disputes, the International Centre for the Settlement of Investment Disputes ("ICSID"). ICSID is an autonomous international organization with close links to the World Bank. While there are other frameworks under which state-investor arbitration occur, for introductory purposes, we'll focus on ICSID.

No general right to investor-state arbitration exists. With respect to ICSID, there are three jurisdictional requirements. First, both parties must have consented to arbitrate or conciliate pursuant to ICSID Rules. Second, one party must be a contracting state, and the other party must be a national of a different contracting state. Third, the dispute must be a legal dispute arising directly out of an investment.

A. Consent

As with any form of arbitration that we have been discussing, parties only have to engage in investor-state arbitration if they have consented to do so. Arbitration is a choice to opt out of the public courts and commit to resolve disputes in arbitration.

The fact that a country is a party to the ICSID Convention does not automatically mean that it has made that choice and commitment. Instead, consent to arbitrate must be found elsewhere. It could be found in a contract between the host country and the investor that contains an arbitration clause, or it could be found in the host country's national legislation. It might also be found in an investment treaty, such as a bilateral investment treaty (BIT) between the host nation and the home country of the investor.

The critical point is that consent to arbitrate must be found, and the mere fact that a country has signed the ICSID Convention does not suffice to prove consent.

B. A Dispute Between Contracting State and a National of a Different Contracting State

The second requirement seems simple enough on its face: one party needs to be a contracting state and the other needs to be an investor from a different contracting state. But things can get complicated in at least two ways.

First, things are tricky when the party to the investment agreement in the host country is not the contracting state itself but rather a subdivision of the contracting state or a state-owned enterprise. For instance, imagine that Country Q, a developing nation, has signed the ICSID Convention and a BIT with the U.S. Katrina Bennett, a rich U.S. investor, wants to build a new factory in Country Q. She partners with Q-State Factory Company, a state-owned enterprise in Country Q, and enters into a concession agreement with Queens County, the largest regional subdivision of Country Q. A dispute breaks out between Katrina, Queens County and Q-State Factory Company. Katrina wants to initiate arbitration. Can she?

It depends. The contracting state must designate to ICSID that the constituent subdivision or agency is subject to its jurisdiction. Additionally, the contracting state must indicate its approval to the consent of the subdivision or agency or notify ICSID that state approval isn't needed. Accordingly, an investor dealing with a subdivision or state-enterprise needs to include in its arbitration clause a provision that ensures these requirements are met.

Second, the investor's nationality can sometimes be hard to pin down. This is particularly true when the investor creates a local incorporated entity in the host country but retains ownership and control of that entity from abroad. Sometimes, because local laws or regulations require it, an investor will incorporate a subsidiary in the host state, which will serve as the vehicle for its investment in that state. But when this occurs, what's the nationality of the subsidiary-investor? Does this local incorporation defeat ICSID jurisdiction?

To deal with this problem, the ICSID Convention provides that a " 'National of another Contracting State' means . . . any juridical person . . . which, because of foreign control, the parties have agreed should be treated as a national of another Contracting State for the purposes of this Convention."[13] While this provision helps, it does not completely solve the problem. In the absence of a clear indication of "agreement" about the nationality of the investor, things can still be messy.

C. _A Legal Dispute Arising out of an Investment_

The ICSID Convention, perplexingly, does not define either legal disputes or investments. Nevertheless, for a dispute to be resolved under the Convention, it must be legal and arise out of an investment.

Courts and tribunals around the world tend to take a very expansive view of both terms. A legal dispute means any fight over a legal right or obligation or any remedy for a breach of a legal obligation. An investment amounts to any project or transaction having economic value.

---

[13]   ICSID Convention art. 25(2)(b).

4. Some Criticisms of Investor-State Arbitration

Criticisms of investor-state arbitration are not new, but they have been increasing over the past decade. In particular, these criticisms heated up in the western world as trade representatives were negotiating multilateral trade agreements (for instance, the Trans-Pacific Partnership Agreement (TPP) and the Trans-Atlantic Investment and Partnership Agreement) that included clauses mandating that disputes arising under the treaties would be resolved via investor-state arbitration.

Cataloguing all of the criticisms would be well beyond the scope of this Guide, but an important goal of this book has been trying to give you tools with which you can assess the pros and cons of arbitration generally.

In general, concerns about investor-state arbitration stem from the belief that public policy disputes about important host-country regulations should not be decided behind closed doors by private individuals who are privately paid. These concerns about investor-state arbitration should seem somewhat familiar, as they track criticisms of domestic arbitration between disparate parties. The demise, in the United States, of subject matter arbitrability coupled with a generous understanding of consent has meant that domestic arbitration now addresses disputes with significant public policy dimensions. Many critics view this state of affairs as cause for concern.

More specifically, controversy around investor-state arbitration clusters around a couple of core problems.

- **Investment disputes are often really political disputes.**

 Investor-state arbitration allows private, foreign parties to question the lawfulness of sensitive policy decisions by host states.

Claims in investor-state arbitration almost always involve challenges to the public acts, and often to the public regulatory acts, of host states. Traditionally, countries have been protected by sovereign immunity for these sorts of acts. The appropriate means of influencing state behavior has traditionally been through the political process. Investor-state arbitration changes all that, making host states potentially liable for actions that could be in the public interest but that negatively impact a rich investor.

In fact, investor-state arbitration tends to implicate tricky policy balancing acts and that are quite significant to local citizens, such as such as the allocation of natural resources, environmental regulation, hazardous waste disposal, taxation, financial regulation, public procurement, official corruption, utilities provision, public transportation, preservation of cultural heritage, discrimination and workers' rights, and healthcare. Moreover, the sorts of regulatory shifts that trigger investor-state arbitrations often occur in connection regime changes. Such changes may be caused by social or economic upheavals in the host country related to citizen's feelings that their interests have not been appropriately taken into account.

In short, investment disputes regularly occur in highly politicized environments, with investors challenging political and policy decisions made by host countries. Citizens in the host countries might see investor-state arbitrations as imperiling governance, bypassing democratic processes or undercutting constitutional protections.

• **The investor-state arbitration process may systematically advantage investors.**

Many critics have argued that investor-state arbitration allows investors to get rich at the expense of ordinary citizens. Pro-investor treaties or local laws are negotiated, often by one set of political actors in a host country, without full support of citizens. Even if the authors of such laws or treaties get thrown out of office, once agreed to, the pro-investor protections get locked in by the threat of arbitration and huge damages awards.

Moreover, investor-state arbitration is a private, for-profit dispute resolution mechanism. Investors are systematically advantaged, according to some critics, because they have a ready mechanism to enforce their rights, money to vindicate those rights, and the potential of huge damages to be paid out of public tax coffers motivating them. Moreover, highly-compensated, elite lawyers specializing in investor-state arbitration have an evident self-interest in encouraging claims in order to grow investor-state arbitration as a business. Similarly, arbitrators specializing in investor-state disputes have an incentive to expand foreign investors' rights and arbitrators' power.

• **The investor-state arbitration process may be too opaque.**

Although ICSID awards are published, some critics worry that investor-state arbitration remains too opaque. Given the quintessentially public nature of many of the issues at stake in investor-state arbitration, transparency may require more than simply providing access to final decisions or even open hearings.

On-going efforts are underway to make the entire investor-state arbitration process, including the process of negotiating and entering into pro-investor treaties, more open and transparent, providing citizens in host countries with opportunities for comments and participation. At present, however, these transparency efforts are largely aspirational.